HOW TO LIVE BETTER ON LESS

A Guide for Waste Watchers

How to Live Better on Less

A GUIDE FOR WASTE WATCHERS

BARBARA JURGENSEN

Illustrated by
AUDREY F. TEEPLE

Augsburg Publishing House
Minneapolis, Minnesota

Contents

Appreciation

A special thanks to these people and organizations:

Nora and Cliff Dahlin

Marie and Christine Hauville

Jean Horn Swanson

Ron Peterson

Dagmar Jurgensen

Marie and Mark Welsh

Dick, Jan and Peter Jurgensen

The Cooperative Extension Service of the University of Illinois College of Agriculture

The Peoples Gas Company

The U.S. Department of Agriculture

Commonwealth Edison

Montgomery Ward

The Subcommittee on Energy of the Committee on Science and Astronautics, U.S. House of Representatives, Ninety-Third Congress

The National Wildlife Federation

The University of Chicago

Corncobs, Firewood and Oats

At the turn of the century when grandpa needed fuel to heat his home, he went out to his woodlot and cut down a few venerable old oaks, filling the air with the good smell of wood. A strong fence around the woods kept the cows out so that new seedlings could spring up and grow and replace the trees he'd cut down. The wood supply never faltered.

Grandma got the big old cookstove going quickly in the morning for frying breakfast bacon and pancakes and heating up the kitchen by throwing in some corncobs. There were tons more out in the shed; and every year, after the corn shelling, she had a new supply.

When they hitched up the team for the wagon trip to town, the horses ran on the oats Grandpa grew.

Today we depend on electricity, gas, and oil to the total equivalent of 2,700 gallons of gasoline per person per year. If we keep on doubling our energy consumption every 15 to 20 years as we have ever since World War II, that will rise to over 7,500 gallons per year per person by the turn of the century. It's too bad that coal, gas, and oil can't replace themselves like trees and corncobs and oats.

Clearly we can't go on as we have been in our use of fuels; by now we all know that we've been using too much.

Food, too, presents a problem. Grandpa and Grandma's farm supplied them with food as well as fuel; from their fields, gardens, and orchards came fresh fruits and vegetables, grains, meat, and eggs. They went to the grocery store only for flour, sugar, coffee, and a few other items that they couldn't produce at home.

Today their grandchildren's greatest effort at raising their own food is probably putting a pot of parsley on the patio.

The earth is the Lord's and the fulness thereof.
David

We know that many people in our world are undernourished; we know that every day some die for lack of good food. And we know that other nations are beginning to want some of the steaks and chops that we have long taken for granted. Can there be world peace without sharing?

Over the years we've said, "We won't worry about food or fuel shortages; when the time comes that we really run low, science will solve the problem for us."

We hoped that solar energy would come to our rescue. But in December 1972 a panel created by the National Science Foundation and the National Aeronautics and Space Administration meeting at the University of Chicago estimated that even by the year 1985 solar energy will be heating and cooling, at the most, 1% of the buildings in this country. Not until the year 2000 do they expect us to be equipped to use solar energy in as many as 10% of our buildings.

In the 1960s we looked forward to the '70s as the era when nuclear energy would solve our fuel crisis. But at present, nuclear energy is filling only 1% of our fuel needs, and the panel saw no prospects for any significant increase.

We hoped to harness the tides, the currents of the sea, the wind, hydrogen from sea water, the heat in the center of the earth—and hopefully we will some day. But the panel saw none of these as offering any real help now or in the immediately foreseeable future.

And our gains in food production are beginning to backfire—overuse of chemical fertilizers, pesticides, and herbicides is wearing out our once-fertile soil.

Clearly we can no longer expect the utility companies to go on doubling their output every 15 years or so—and they're partly responsible for our dilemma: after encouraging us to buy more appliances and use more of their products, they suddenly tell us that they can't keep up with our demands.

Nor can we expect science to bail us out from our extravagance.

Abruptly the overabundance seems to have vanished. We're running lower on food and fuel; and neither science nor industry is able to come up with the help we need.

Now we're going to have to learn to live with what we have; we're going to have to scale our demands down to the way things are.

All of this is hard for most of us to realize. Many of us were brought up during a time when American industry was encouraging us to consume as much as possible to make jobs for everyone. Eat! Drink! Drive your car! Consume! You almost felt guilty if you weren't out spending your money.

Now that day has passed and we've entered a new day—the dawning, perhaps, of the Age of Scarcity.

How does one live in a time of scarcity? Many of us have never experienced it. Some have—those who lived through the Depression of the '30s and the rationing days of World War II and those who grew up in economically-depressed areas or impoverished segments of society. But for many of us it will be a totally new experience.

How will we react? Some will feel sorry for themselves and refuse to cooperate. Others will refuse to admit there's a problem and will go on as they were before. Still others will take it as a challenge to be met, an adventure, a test of what they're made of.

It can be a good time for examining our way of life. What are we living for after all—merely to feed and clothe and shelter ourselves?

Is there more to life than living for things?

When Jesus said, "I have come so that you may have life and have it more abundantly," he was inviting us to a different way of living— one of being loved, then of loving and sharing and being concerned.

The Christian church has sometimes been blamed for ecological problems, for encouraging man to have dominion over the earth. But

● ● ●

Simplify, simplify, simplify. Thoreau

surely God didn't intend for us to misuse our soil, air, and water. When he gave us dominion over the earth, he expected us to care for it.

The Christian viewpoint on our use of the earth can be summed up in five points:

1. Everything belongs to God—we merely used it while we're here.
2. We should use no more than our share.
3. We should try to see that everyone gets his share.
4. We should keep things in balance, putting back as well as taking.
5. We should leave the world in good shape for those who will come after us.

Can we make the changes that will be necessary to live this way—

Can we stop thinking in terms of *increasing* our standard of living?

Can we say, "This is enough—I already have enough gadgets and appliances"?

Can we realize it's no longer true that "there's plenty more where this came from"?

Can we cut down on conspicuous consumption, on being so concerned with making a big impression?

Can we talk manufacturers into changing from planned obsolescence to making goods that will last?

Perhaps we can adopt the old New England way of conserving things:

 Use it up;
Wear it out;
Make it do;
Do without.

We may make some great discoveries as we embark on this more sensible way of living—

We may find that less is better, that the fewer possessions we have, the more time we have for neighborliness and friendliness.

We may find that our consciences feel better when we aren't clasping so many of the world's goods to ourselves.

We may find that we feel healthier with our homes a little less hot in the winter and a little less cold in the summer, that walking or riding a bicycle feels good, that we're more comfortable when we don't overeat.

We may find that simpler living has fewer pressures, that we feel more relaxed when we aren't living so much for things, that living in tune with nature is its own reward.

12

The Five R's

Back in frontier days great-grandmother and great-grandfather made almost everything themselves: when they butchered they saved the tallow for making soap and candles; they sheared their own sheep, carded the wool, spun it into yarn, and knit it into the family's stockings, mittens, scarves, and caps.

They kept the family loom busy weaving materials for dresses, coats, and pants; they raised up houses, barns, and sheds from whatever materials were available—sod, logs, mud, or stone; and they produced almost everything the family ate—spicy sausages, fresh eggs, tangy apple butter, juicy strawberries, golden pumpkin pies.

Very little was wasted. Great-grandma cut worn-out clothes into strips and braided them into rugs. She sewed scraps of new cloth into quilts in a fascinating array of designs, and she fashioned the family's undergarments from flour sacks.

Great-grandpa resoled shoes on the iron last that was a part of almost every household. He dug the potatoes, carrots, beets, and turnips and stacked them away in the earthy-smelling family root cellar. And if he couldn't make the house snug for winter, he had no one to blame for his chilblains but himself.

Life might have been hard in some ways, but they had the satisfaction of creating things with their own hands and of using their ingenuity to provide for the needs of their family.

But gradually, as they moved off the farm and into the city, they no longer had to use these old skills and there was no occasion to teach them to their children or their children's children, and so the skills were forgotten.

Now, with the world's rapidly expanding population and dwindling supply of natural resources—and because we're tiring of plastic manufactured products that all look the same—we may want to relearn some of these old ways of doing things.

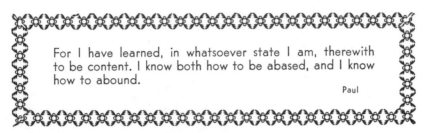

For I have learned, in whatsoever state I am, therewith to be content. I know both how to be abased, and I know how to abound.

Paul

REPAIR IT

Many things that a person at first glance might be tempted to throw out can often be fixed rather quickly and easily. The ceiling light fixture that breaks when you're replacing a burned-out bulb can usually be glued back together with epoxy. Follow the directions on the package, then set the fixture somewhere out of the way to dry. When you put it back up, it should be as strong as it was before it broke.

In fact, with epoxy and a few other glues you can fix almost anything that breaks around the house. The knob on your TV snaps in two? Wrap ordinary sewing thread around the base of it many times, then coat the wrapping with epoxy and let it dry. A coffee table loses a leg? Find the appropriate glue and put it back in place. The wallpaper in the bathroom is coming loose? Ditto.

If you put your mind to it, there are few things that come apart around the house that you can't put back together again.

A handyman's book can sometimes be a big help. A good one will have chapters on all the main maintenance crises that can arise in the average home. There'll be pictures, diagrams and clear instructions. Lean heavily on it.

After you've mastered the art of gluing, consider the washer, the round rubber thing whose wearing out makes faucets drip. Buy a package of assorted sizes, unscrew the faucet, remove the old one, and insert the new. This can save you a lot of hot water: one dripping faucet can waste as much as 650 gallons of hot water a year.

Your county agent and county home extension agent have free pamphlets on making many types of home repairs as well as on just about anything else you might want to know about running a home. Call and ask them to send you some in your particular areas of interest, or visit their office and pick out the ones that interest you most. If you live in a large metropolitan area, call the local office of the extension division of the university of your state.

There's a good feeling in being able to take care of yourself and your family. Our ancestors took great pride in their self-reliance.

So before throwing anything out, ask yourself, *"Is there any way I can fix it?"*

RE-USE IT

In order to live well amid shortages (and to develop creative thinking in your family), make a game of asking, *"What are we in the habit of throwing away that could be used again?"*

Instead of tossing out that old card table with a badly-scratched top, buy some colorful contact paper and cover it. You may find it's more attractive than it was when it was new.

Or you might ask yourself which of the disposable items you use around the house wouldn't have to be disposed of quite so often. One family re-uses the paper bag in their vacuum cleaner by cutting open the end farthest from the motor, folding it several times and securing it with paper clips. When it's full they remove the paper clips, unfold the end and empty it, then refold and reclip. They've been using the same bag for over a year and think it may still be good for quite a while yet.

They also got to thinking, after moving, that it would be a waste to throw out all the boxes. After asking among their friends, they found another family due to move soon that was happy to come and pick them all up.

As someone could have said,

> He who doesn't throw away
> Can re-use another day.

Economy is the art of making the most of life.
George Bernard Shaw

RECLAIM IT

Besides repairing and re-using, reclaiming is another way of avoiding discarding something that would have to be replaced. Whenever you encounter a problem of wear in a household item, ask yourself, *"Is there any way this item could possibly be reclaimed?"*

When Stan and Sue moved into an older home, there was a shag carpet running through the living room, dining room, and hall. Also running through the living room, dining room and hall was a well-worn path that had no shagginess whatsoever left to it. After trying various things, they found that a wire brush—the kind painters use to remove old paint—could be used to bring the nap up again.

They also found that the linoleum in the areas of heaviest traffic in the kitchen was so worn down that the dark brown lines forming the arabesque pattern were completely gone. All that was left in front of the sink, stove, and refrigerator was the yellow background.

Their first thought was to rip it all out. But it seemed such a waste when most of the linoleum was still in very good shape.

A few days later when one of the children was in the kitchen using a dark brown magic marker to make a poster, Sue warned, "Be careful not to drop the marker on the floor—we'd probably never get the marks up."

Then it struck her—if the magic marker would be that hard to get off the floor . . .

She borrowed the marker and drew in one of the lines that had worn off the linoleum, waited a few minutes for it to dry, then tried washing it off. It stayed there, so she kept going until she had all the missing design drawn in. When she finished, it was almost impossible to tell that any part of the design had ever been worn.

That was almost a year ago, and the lines are beginning to wear a little now in some spots, but Sue can redraw them in just a few minutes.

And they found that a dark blue magic marker was just the thing to touch up the worn places in their bedroom carpet and restore the color.

In the last century our great-grandparents staked their claims; now it's time for us to reclaim.

RESTORE IT

For many years we seem to have been in a headlong rush to buy, buy, buy. The magazine *Better Homes & Gardens* has described itself to potential advertisers as "the magazine for people with BUY on their minds."

Hopefully we're reaching a more mature stage in which we'll ask ourselves, *"Instead of buying something new, where can I find something that I can restore to usefulness?"*

Mary and Bill's home looks like the house-of-the-month in one of the top decorator magazines: they have brass beds that they've restored, handsome old antique chests, fascinating light fixtures, interesting old mirrors, quaint old brass-bound trunks. They have a favorite Saturday afternoon recreation that not too many people would care for, but they enjoy it: they play "Go to the Dump."

"The kids would rather do this on a Saturday afternoon than anything else," Mary says. "We've covered all the good places in a 50-mile radius several times, and there's always something new each time we go back. We don't always come up with treasures, but that's what makes it fun—the fact that we *might* find something really exciting."

Other families keep an eye open for what townspeople put out by the street on trash day—an aluminum lawn chair that needs rewebbing, a tricycle that could use a coat of paint, an end table that needs refinishing.

In towns that have a week each spring when householders can clean out their basements, attics, and garages and put out anything smaller than an automobile, there can be some interesting things—a TV that only needs a few new tubes, a wheelbarrow that needs new handles, a very good lamp that needs rewiring.

There are many treasures to be had for little or nothing by anyone willing to put in a little time restoring.

He that is rich need not live sparingly, and he that can live sparingly need not be rich.

Benjamin Franklin

REACTIVATE IT

Another good way of stimulating creative thinking in the family is to ask, the next time the family needs something, *"What do we already have around the house that we could press into service to fill this particular need?"*

Phyllis and Craig started asking themselves this question instead of hurrying out to the store to buy things. When they needed a bookcase, they looked around till they found some boards up in the rafters of the garage. They gave them a coat of maple stain and stacked them up with some bricks they found piled up next to the garage.

When they needed a desk, they looked again and found an unused flush door in the basement. After staining it to match the bookcase, they placed a filing cabinet under one end and some pieces of old lumber, stained maple, for legs under the other.

When the window shades were in need of replacing, Phyllis looked through her box of fabric remnants, found some striped material that looked good with the maple furniture, cut it to the right size, sewed a seam at the bottom to make a place for the wooden piece to slide in, tacked the fabric onto the rollers and had some very attractive shades.

When the floor needed a rug, they found an old trunk in the attic full of discarded wool suits and coats. They cut these into strips, sewed the strips together and wound them into large balls, then started braiding. This became a family project that they worked on in the evening, braiding, then laying it out on a table, and sewing it together. The rug they created is beautiful and rich looking and should last many, many years.

Then they needed lamps. In the basement were some interesting pieces of driftwood they'd picked up the previous summer. They mounted these on some small pieces of lumber, fitted on parts from lamp kits, then added shades.

Phyllis has made a lot of things with remnants of cloth: arm covers for the davenport and chairs, new covers for the sofa pillows, dustcovers for the toaster and mixer, guest towels, dinner napkins, place mats, dresser scarves, aprons—as well as many children's clothes.

When she needed bedspreads for the two bunk beds, she found that the small spread for a bunk cost as much as one that was almost twice as large that was intended for a double bed. So she bought a double-bed size, cut it in two, and seamed up the raw edges (this took about twenty minutes) and had two spreads for the price of one.

She's made blankets from mill ends, sewn together carpet samples to make a rug for the children's room, and made all sorts of things from odds and ends of fabric she's pieced together in attractive crazy-quilt designs.

To add the finishing touch, they've gathered interesting weeds, grasses, seed pods, cones, and whatever else they've found on their walks, making winter bouquets and arrangements. They've found a real challenge in asking themselves, "What do we already have around the house that we could press into service to fill this particular need?"

If you'd like to make your home more interesting and individual without causing more of a drain on the world's already strained resources, remember to ask yourself these five questions:

1. Instead of throwing this item out, is there any way I can fix it?
2. What are we in the habit of throwing away that could be used again?
3. Is there any way this item could possibly be reclaimed?
4. Instead of buying something new, where can I find something that I can restore to usefulness?
5. What do we already have around the house that we can press into service to fill this particular need?

REPAIR IT.
RE-USE IT.
RECLAIM IT.
RESTORE IT.
REACTIVATE IT.

Canning & Freezing

Canning used to be a big family occasion back on the farm. Cousins and aunts and grandmothers came from miles around and helped put the fruits and vegetables into the bottles and onto the fruitroom shelves. The wonderful aroma of apples and cinnamon filled the house. And the spicy smell of pickled peaches.

Grandma found a way for even the preschoolers to help: using some trusty blunt-nosed scissors, they could snip the ends off green or yellow beans, then snap the beans into pieces. Or cut the stems and stiff ribs from spinach. Or dice rhubarb.

Small children also could shell peas, popping an astonishing number into their mouth as they worked. They put a lot of zest into pulling the husks off corn—and they had a lot of fun splashing around (best done outdoors), cleaning carrots and beets in a large tub of water.

As fruit came into season, there were apples for children to wash and pull the stems from; peaches, pears, plums to scrub gently and strawberries to wash and remove the hulls from. The older children were usually given the latter job; somehow the temptation to squeeze the tender red berries sometimes got to be too much for the younger ones.

Canning and freezing can still be a happy family occasion. It's a rare person who doesn't get caught up in the pleasure of working with all these good things that nature has produced so abundantly. And the child who has washed and brushed carrots and shelled the peas is not apt to say, "I don't like vegetables."

Canning used to be a rather hot job. The kitchen billowed clouds of steam—and the super-heated old cookstove didn't add to the comfort. Today's gas and electric ranges with their fans to exhaust steam and heat make the whole process much cooler.

And, now that freezing has become part of our way of life, things are also much easier. Some foods need only be washed, put into a container, and placed in the freezer, although most fruits usually need a little sugar added. In a few hours a family can pack up enough peaches or cherries or strawberries to last a long time.

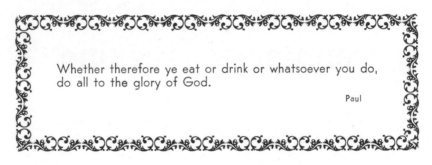

Whether therefore ye eat or drink or whatsoever you do, do all to the glory of God.

Paul

CANNING

Canning isn't hard to learn—many people have learned from a cookbook or from free pamphlets they picked up at their county home-extension agent's office. Others have asked a friend or neighbor who cans to let them help a few times to see how it's done.

If you haven't tried canning, you have a very satisfying experience ahead of you. To see the fruits or vegetables packed like sparkling jewels in a shining glass jar is certainly one of life's elemental pleasures. And to know that the food is there on the shelf and that you canned it yourself can give an uncommon feeling of accomplishment.

In recent years so many more families have decided to try canning that many stores have been running out of jars. If you run into this problem, you might be able to find an older friend whose family is grown who has dozens of jars sitting unused in her fruit cellar. Make her an offer she can't resist.

If members of your family are on special diets, you can do your canning without using salt or sugar—the small amounts of sugar or salt used in canning are not there to help prevent spoilage anyway.

JAMS, JELLIES AND PRESERVES

Many families have found making their own jellies, jams, and preserves an enjoyable activity. There are so many good fruits for this: apples, cherries, grapes, blueberries, peaches, pineapple, plums, currants, strawberries, raspberries—the list is almost endless.

Often you can find a source of fruit without going to the store: you or your neighbors or friends may have fruit that would otherwise go to waste that would make excellent jam or jelly. Or you might pick wild fruit on your walks through the countryside. Or get it relatively inexpensively at a pick-your-own orchard. If you must get it at the grocery, wait for the peak of the season for the best fruit at the best prices.

Once you have the fruit, gather the family around for some of the most interesting proceedings that go on in a kitchen—preparing the juicy red berries, watching them cook, ladling them into hot glasses, sealing them with paraffin or jar lids. The aroma will be heavenly, and the finished product will shimmer like priceless gems.

Many people like to add commercial pectin in liquid or powder form to their berries and sugar. The pectin, made from apples or citrus fruits, shortens the cooking time, gives a larger amount of jam or jelly from the same amount of berries, and makes the whole process just about foolproof. You don't have to wonder if you've cooked the fruit long enough; you just cook it the length of time specified in the enclosed recipes. You can also take out the guesswork by using a jelly, candy, or deep-fat thermometer.

If you get in the habit of saving suitable jars during the year, it won't be necessary to buy special ones for your jam.

Paraffin for sealing the tops can be kept in a tin can in the cupboard. Each time you make jam, heat the can in a pan of hot water; paraffin is very flammable, so never place the can directly on the burner. Whenever you open a jar of jam after that, wash the piece of wax that was on top of it and drop it back into the can for the next melting.

Many people make their own fruit toppings for ice cream by using a basic jam recipe and either cutting down the sugar to two-thirds of what is called for and replacing the other third with water or juice, or by adding one-half cup more fruit, juice, or water to the basic recipe.

For better nutrition, some people like to use honey in canning and in making jams and jellies; honey can usually be substituted for up to half the sugar called for in the recipe. Light, mild-flavored honeys are

23

best for this. Honey will usually make the product a little darker and will change the flavor a little—for the better, honey-lovers say. Many fruits are enhanced by the use of honey rather than sugar; honey seems to blend more naturally with the fruit's own sweetness.

Your father knoweth what things you need.

Jesus

FREEZING

Freezing is one of the simplest and easiest ways of preserving foods at home. It helps fruits and vegetables keep their natural color, fresh flavor, and nutritive values. And, since most of the preparation for the table is done before freezing, it provides foods that are ready to serve on short notice.

Freezing is a good way to make sure a bumper crop of succulent fruits and vegetables isn't wasted. And by doubling the recipe when you prepare one of your family's favorite dishes, you can store enough for another day.

FREEZING VEGETABLES

Tomatoes can be frozen simply by washing and drying them, removing stem ends, and placing them in a plastic bag or box. When you want to use them in a soup, stew, or casserole, hold them under running water and the skins will slip off easily.

Some people place the tomatoes on cookie sheets in the freezer until they're frozen solid, then pack them in bags. That way they stay separate from each other, and only as many as are needed can be removed from the bag.

Green peppers need only be washed and dried, cut into pieces, and deseeded. They, too, can be spread out on a cookie sheet in the freezer until they're frozen solid, then poured into bags, ready to be poured out again in the amount needed.

Other vegetables need to be cooked in boiling water or steam for a few minutes. Check a recipe book for times.

FREEZING FRUIT

Freezing fruit is basically the same as preparing it for serving fresh. Wash it well, cut it into serving pieces if necessary, and add sugar or

24

honey if desired. This added sweetening helps preserve the texture and flavor of some fruits. Ascorbic acid (vitamin C) is also needed to keep some fruits from turning darker in color.

For containers to freeze in choose boxes, bags, jars, aluminum foil, or heavy freezer paper—just be sure they're as moisture-proof as possible. Tests have shown that aluminum foil keeps things from drying out better than freezer paper.

The plastic boxes that margarine and other products come in work well. Glass jars are also good, although not for foods that will be packed in a liquid, which expands when it freezes and may crack them. Peanut butter jars with their wide-mouth tops are worth saving for freezing. The thin plastic wrappers that bread comes in are all right for storing things a very short time, but for longer storage they're not moisture-proof enough.

For best quality, freeze all foods quickly. Never add more than three pounds per cubic foot of the freezer's capacity at any given time. Wait until that batch is solidly frozen before doing another; flavor and texture will be much better.

For we brought nothing into this world, and it is certain we can carry nothing out. And having food and raiment let us be therewith content.

Paul

LIVING WITH A FREEZER

There seem to be two main problems that many of us have with our freezers. One is that things get lost in the icy depths. Pretty soon we don't know what we've got way back down there, and we don't want to drag out everything to find out.

To keep things from getting lost in your freezer, use a large brown paper bag for each type of food and write the name on the bag with a felt tip marker: BREAD or PEACHES or whatever. Then you can arrange the bags alphabetically from left to right. Or arrange foods according to their color—red, orange, yellow, green—from left to right. Or whatever system you find works best for you. With the bags clearly labeled, you can set one on top of another and fill your freezer quite full without anything getting lost.

Some people keep a list of what they have in the freezer and mark off each item as they remove it. This is not necessary if you use the brown bag system. You'll know at a glance how much you have of any given item.

The other problem with freezers is that we have a tendency to put things in and forget them.

Try not to use your freezer as a long-term repository; it's better to keep using up things while they're fresh. A good rule is to use whatever you can from it each day. (Use fresh things in the garden first, of course.) Think of your freezer as a temporary holding place rather than as a Fort Knox to be protected from all withdrawals, and you'll get much better service from it.

And in order to make sure that nothing in the freezer gets too old, plan to use up everything in it once a year. Some people do this before they begin restocking it in the early summer.

Some things should not be kept this long, however. Most breads, rolls, cakes, and many meats should be used before two or three months. Ice cream and sherbet should be used up in a month.

A full freezer gives you more economical operation, so don't buy one so large that it will never be full.

Chest-type freezers are the least costly to run because their door is on the top. Those with a door on the front lose a lot of cold air every time they're opened.

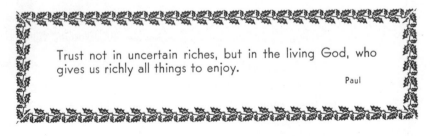

Trust not in uncertain riches, but in the living God, who gives us richly all things to enjoy.

Paul

DRYING FRUITS

Some families have found drying fruit an interesting experience. And this is a good thing to do if you've bought a lot of plums or cherries or other fruit and you can see that they aren't all going to be eaten fresh.

Wash the fruit and spread it out on cookie sheets in the sun to dry, shaking it loose several times a day to make sure each piece dries on all sides.

A covering of cheesecloth will help keep out birds and insects. If small neighbors begin to upset the project, it can be moved indoors to a window sill, to the oven (turn it on to a low heat for a few minutes, then turn it off, leaving the fruit in), or to the top of the refrigerator near the back. The heat coming up from the back of the refrigerator will speed the drying process.

When the fruit has reached the desired state of dryness, wash off any bits of mold that might have formed, dry it, and place it in glass jars or plastic bags.

Children enjoy watching this whole process and may find the product so delectable along the way that you won't have too much left to store.

The Car

A few years ago when there was talk of selecting a national flower, someone suggested that we make it a carnation—because that's what we seem to be, a car-nation.

Grandpa with his horse and buggy would be mighty dismayed to come back and see how we've polluted our air with exhaust fumes, our waters with oil, and our land with piles of discarded cars.

As a nation we've become devoted to the highway and horsepower, with the car serving not only as a status symbol for many people but as an extension of their personalities. We can't go on the way we have been, but it's not going to be easy to change.

Limiting the size of automobiles will cut significantly the amount of energy and materials consumed both in building and in maintaining a car. Some people say, "I wouldn't feel safe on the highway in a small car. I might get pulverized by a bigger car." But if *no one* is out on the highway in a large car, no one needs a large car for protection.

Taxing large cars heavily will provide revenue for ecological uses, but this extra revenue may be eaten up by the problems the larger cars cause. As long as we continue to build cars with engines insatiable for gasoline, we're probably going to have more problems than we can handle. Hopefully the large car, like the dinosaur, is a thing of the past.

It's time our society stops admiring the person who indulges himself with a huge car and starts admiring the person who shows his concern for his fellow human beings by buying a small car and using it only when necessary.

In ages past our literature celebrated heroes who rode: "Paul Revere's Ride," "Into the valley of death rode the 600," "The Ride of the Valkyrie." What we need today are poems and operas and songs celebrating *today's* hero—the person who *resists* the urge to jump in the car and go for a ride.

If we as car users are concerned about conserving fuel, here are some things that can help:

Buy a smaller car next time. "Small" no longer means "cheaply made." Small cars have some real advantages: their initial cost is less; they give more miles per gallon; repairing them is less expensive; they're easier to drive and easier to find a parking space for; and their insurance and licenses are more reasonable.

If you have two cars, use the smaller one for running errands and save gas.

Cut down to one car if you can. Or none. Have you ever considered how pleasant it might be not to have to think of getting the car oiled and greased, winterized, summerized, tuned-up, overhauled, painted, washed, waxed, polished, cleaned, and undercoated? Have you thought of how much time and money you would save if you didn't have to buy new tires, get the wheels balanced and aligned, replace the muffler and tailpipe, put in new turning lights, have the valves reground, and get the dents removed and the fenders unbent? Aren't you just a little tired of cleaning out the trunk, changing flat tires in the middle of nowhere, sweeping out the garage, and making those big car payments every month? Be the first in your block to be carfree and carefree.

Abundance is no longer an assured way of life.
Norman Cousins

Be a public transportation booster. Whenever you can, use public instead of private transit. Your city may not raise a statue in honor of you, the unknown citizen who conserved fuel, but you'll have the good feeling of knowing you did what you could.

✠

Learn the schedules and routes of public transportation near you so you can make good use of it. If it doesn't meet your needs, encourage additional routing and scheduling.

✠

Have you considered that great invention, the taxi? Possibly you could get along without a car by using public transportation whenever possible, calling a taxi when necessary. It's a lot cheaper than owning a car.

✠

Motorcycles use very little gas.

✠

How are you with a bicycle? Don't laugh—you may be missing a lot of good, healthy, invigorating fun. A bicycle has been called the most efficient human/machine combination; nothing surpasses it as a means of transportation. Bicycling is one of the most enjoyable ways of getting and/or keeping your weight under control. Pedaling a bicycle not only helps stimulate the circulation; the pedaling motion actually helps to pump the blood through the body. Mental fatigue can be relieved by bicycling. After the emotional tensions of a busy day, bicycling along a quiet country road or through a city park can help you feel more relaxed.

✠

A bicycle with three wheels is excellent for those who worry about balancing a two-wheeler. The large basket between the wheels provides space for groceries, laundry or other items.

✠

A one-speed bike—like the one you had when you were young—is good for in-town transportation. And you won't lose as much if it's stolen. Also it's not as apt to be stolen.

✠

The two-speed bicycle is a good compromise between the less efficient one-speed and the more expensive three-speed. It's also less complicated than a three-speed: to change the speed you back-pedal until the brakes start to grab; then, before the bicycle begins to slow down, start pedaling forward again, this time in the new gear.

✠

If you can operate an electric egg beater, you can learn to ride a three-speed bicycle. If you're going to be riding much, the increase in price will be offset by the increased efficiency and enjoyment. A three-speed lets you ride greater distances with less effort; if there are hills, you'll have fewer problems getting up them.

※

A five-speed bicycle lets you travel longer distances without getting tired. Steep hills are more of a problem than with a ten-speed, but with a tail wind or down long hills you can go fairly fast.

✛

Ten-speeds are very efficient. Many cyclists do 150 miles a day on them touring the country. The cheapest ten-speeds aren't worth the money; the better ones are expensive. To get to know a ten-speed, you'll need to ride a lot.

✛

Many states have laws governing bicycle equipment. Lights and reflectors are usually required for night riding—and you shouldn't ride without them anyway.

✛

In addition to a light and a reflector, side reflectors will make you safer riding at night.

※

Audible warning devices are often required—these can include the human voice. Whatever you choose, it should be something that will warn people of your presence rather than scare them. If a pedestrian is crossing the road and doesn't see you, you don't need to make his hair stand on end to alert him to your approach. Frightening those on foot can give bicyclists a bad image. The best warning device is the bicycle bell: people recognize it and know a bicycle is coming.

※

Baskets for over the front or rear wheel of the bicycle are handy.

✛

Encourage the development of bike trails in your area.

> Man must be disappointed with the lesser things of life before he can comprehend the greater.
> Bulwer-Lytton

Have you discovered the pleasures of walking? When did you last hike far enough to feel revitalized from head to toe?

⊹

Never drive your car if you can take public transportation. Never take public transportation if you can walk.

⊹

When you drive, use all the means you know to conserve gasoline:
1. Reduce your speed, and get more miles per gallon.
2. Tell the gas station attendant, "Fill it *almost* up" instead of "Fill it up." Gas can expand from the heat and spill over—especially if you're parked on an incline.
3. Don't buy gasoline with a higher octane rating than necessary. The newer cars run on regular gas.
4. Drive smoothly. Fast acceleration is a big gas waster.
5. When you see a stop sign ahead, don't speed up to get more of a kick out of putting on the brakes. (It's surprising how many people do this.) Instead let your car slow down before you apply the brakes.
6. When you're caught in the rush hour crawl on an expressway, keep your eye on the traffic ahead and let the car slow down easily instead of continually hitting the brakes.
7. Don't speed away from a light only to have to wait at the next one. Look ahead and pace your driving so you'll have a smooth ride uninterrupted by constant stops and starts.
8. Don't race the engine. If it idles poorly, it may need a tune-up.

✠

To get the most from each gallon of gas, get your car engine tuned every 6000 miles.

⊹

Keep your tires properly inflated; underinflated tires decrease gas mileage.

⊹

Instead of warming up the engine completely while standing still, drive slowly for the first mile.

⊹

Never idle the motor more than three minutes while waiting for someone or something.

⊹

Except for winding your way through the mountains, don't accelerate to go up hills. Rather keep a steady speed—you'll gradually pick up the momentum you need.

☩

Change the oil every 3000 to 6000 miles. A sludgy engine starts slowly and doesn't have as much power.

✠

If you keep your car in good repair from bumper to bumper you won't be so anxious to trade it in. (The country already has enough junked cars.) Consider the neighbor who gets the urge now and then to trade his car in: he gets busy and puts it in A-1 shape to get the best possible price for it—and when he's done it always looks so good that he decides to keep it.

☩

Europeans don't seem to have gotten caught up in the headlong rush many Americans have to trade cars every few years. Said one, "If we can't make our cars last ten years, we think there's something wrong with us."

☩

If we keep our cars longer, we'll save raw materials and the energy used in manufacturing—and we won't have to establish so many new junkyards.

☩

When you do need to buy a new car, make fuel consumption a major consideration.

☩

Do without as many optional electrical features on your new car as you can.

✠

Air conditioning units and automatic transmissions increase fuel consumption. A car without automatic shift gives several more miles to the gallon.

☩

Drive without your air conditioning on whenever possible. At highway speeds it may not be needed—or if you travel at the cooler times of day.

☩

Keep rust removed from bumpers, headlights, and trim; paint rusty spots on the body immediately. Your car appreciates a little first aid as much as you would.

✠

When you wash your car at home, use a nozzle with a shut-off control to save water.

✛

Perhaps your car is leaving a trail of smoke that you, in the driver's seat, can't see. The next time you leave the house, have someone check.

✛

If you change the oil in your car yourself, don't dump it on the ground or pour it on the driveway to hold down the dust. Most of it will run off with the rain and eventually end up polluting our rivers and lakes. Instead take it for recycling to the station where you buy gas.

✛

Salt is very hard on cars as well as on the environment. The amount of salt used by some cities on icy streets causes more than $100 worth of damage per year to the average car. Sand would be better in many ways.

✠

When you must go somewhere in your car, invite others to ride with you. Two passengers are better than one—and three or four are absolutely marvelous. That trip to the store or church will also be more pleasant in the company of friends.

✛

Instead of making many trips, consolidate all the tasks requiring an auto into one trip.

✛

Plan where you're going before you start out so you don't retrace your steps.

✛

Don't hop in and out of your car, making many stops in a small area —park in a central location.

✠

Instead of driving around for ten or fifteen minutes looking for a parking spot, be willing to park a little farther away and walk a few blocks.

✠

Instead of driving to the other side of the city to the doctor, dentist, and piano teacher, ask around until you find a capable doctor, dentist, or teacher in your immediate area that you can perhaps even walk to. (Note to mothers who put in long hours driving their kids around: Is this trip really necessary? Perhaps the energy crisis gives you the reason you've been looking for to tell the kids to walk or take their bikes.)

❖

Organize car pools for getting to work and to functions that meet regularly. You'll save money on gas, tolls, and parking. With fewer cars on the road, you'll get to where you're going faster, and help the environment.

✢

Also organize ad hoc car pools for special occasions. Ad hoc car pools can be put together to go to this place or that; to this party, to that outing; to this program, to that game. Better one car than five or six.

✢

Get a grocery cart so you can walk to the store.

✢

Perhaps some day people won't move so often or to such distant places. Moving vans log a lot of miles.

✢

Don't buy all-terrain vehicles. People had a lot of fun before snowmobiles and dunebuggies and the like polluted the environment with smoke and noise.

❖

Instead of spending your entire vacation traveling, go one place and stay there.

✢

Buses consume the least energy per passenger mile, then trains, cars, planes. Measured in British Thermal Units, they use the following amounts of energy per passenger mile:

Buses	—	2500
Trains	—	4000
Cars	—	7000
Planes	—	9800

✢

Try vacationing around home. Most of us have a number of places not too far from our house that we've planned to visit some day but just haven't gotten to because they're so close that we haven't thought we needed to make a special effort. Now is the time to explore them. You'll find many advantages: no packing of suitcases; no loading the car impossibly full; no long, hot, tiring drives across endless wastes; no scurrying to find a motel or camping spot before nightfall (and no huge motel and restaurant bills); no souvenir shops to steer the kids clear of (they certainly won't be tempted to look through souvenir shops in their own home town); no need to find someone to water the plants, walk the dog, feed the cat, clean the gerbils; no need to stop the mail, newspaper or milk deliveries; no need to worry about burglars.

Explore your own back yard. Instead of driving hither and yon looking for interesting things, take time to look carefully at some of the wonders right at your doorstep.

Some psychologists are predicting that restrictions on automobile travel may cause some people to feel quite depressed. Those who have been in the habit of jumping into the car and hitting the road to work off the frustrations of the week will need to find new ways to get rid of their pent-up emotions. Walking may be just the thing. It's better than driving in several ways: a person gets very little exercise sitting behind the wheel, and the car does add to pollution; a person walking refreshes his whole being without harming the environment. And in the car you never get close enough to nature to see what's really happening, while on foot you can keep a close tab on the opening of the leaves on the bushes and trees, the progress of the birds in their nest-building, the progress of your neighbors in their gardening.

Someday we'll probably look back and say, "Remember when we used to *drive* everywhere?" And we'll look and feel better, from doing more walking.

• • •

There is more to life than increasing its speed.
Gandhi

Clothing

Grandma had one good outfit—a ruffly, long-sleeved white blouse and a long, dark skirt. In the winter she added a shawl. In the summer she was rather warm.

Today our closets are something to behold. Do we really need all those clothes? Every garment that we buy requires a great expenditure of energy in producing the fiber, spinning it into yarn or thread, weaving or knitting it into fabric, sewing it into a dress or suit or lounging robe—plus all the transportation to get it from the field to the factory to the department store. If we only bought half as many clothes, half this energy could be saved.

Are we, after all, clothes racks or people? Many of the best-dressed men and women have very few clothes; they've found that a few carefully chosen clothes are all they need. And the person who simplifies his wardrobe will have that much more time and money to spend on more important things. For the person who often wishes he had a little more to give to really worthwhile causes, here is a possible place to get it.

A good thing to do when each new season approaches is to check your closet first. Instead of rushing out to buy new clothes, see what you already have that's still wearable, what needs a little repair, and what should be given away. You may find that you have all the clothes you really need.

When you do go out to buy a new garment, try to buy something that is so basic and well-designed that you'll be able to wear it for several years. Women can accessorize with scarves, pins, necklaces, and blouses; men can give their basic wardrobe variety with shirts, ties, and belts.

If you're buying clothes for a special occasion, select something that you can wear again on other occasions so it doesn't just hang in your closet.

Sometimes a slight change in a dress you've tired of can make it wearable again—new buttons, a new belt, new costume jewelry, a little jacket or vest to wear over it.

If you want to avoid that unhappy moment of going to the closet and finding nothing to wear, try this: reserve one end of your closet for garments that need to go to the cleaners, and a space next to it for those that need repairs. Don't leave any garments needing either cleaning or repairs in with your other clothes; then you'll know that whatever is in the main part of your closet is wearable.

This system also makes it easier when you go to the cleaners; you'll have the garments all ready. And when you have some free time, you'll have those that need repairing already gathered together. If you keep your clothes cleaned and in good repair, you won't be so tempted to go out and buy new ones.

Confusion in the family coat closet can be avoided by putting a shoe box for each family member (with his name on it) on the shelf. Each person can then keep track of his own gloves, scarves, and hats. This keeps these small items from getting mislaid and having to be replaced.

> Conform thyself to thy present fortune, and cut thy coat according to thy cloth.
>
> R. Burton

When it comes time to launder the family clothes, here are some tips that can help conserve energy and money:

WASHING

Wait until you have enough clothes and linens to make a good-sized load; don't run many small batches.

✠

Instead of doing all sheets in one load and all small items in the next, put half of each in each load. Having a variety of sizes of things in a load allows freer circulation and increases the cleaning action.

✠

If you must wash a small load, use the small load setting on the washer.

✠

Get the right size washer for your needs.

✠

Do our clothes really need to be washed so often? Many times all that is needed is a little de-spotting.

✠

And do our clothes really need to be a blinding white? Is it worth ruining our environment to keep them that way?

✠

The major cost in washing clothes is the hot water. The more you can wash with cold or warm water cycles, the more energy and money you'll save. First sort the loads according to fabrics and how soiled they are. Permanent-press items need only warm water; lightly soiled items often can be washed with warm instead of hot water; cool or cold water can be used for woolens. There are a number of cold-water soaps available.

✠

Using cold water for the rinse cycle helps colored clothes retain their color, keeps washable woolens from shrinking, and helps minimize wrinkling in wash-and-wear articles.

✠

Use the shortest cycle, lowest water level, and lowest temperature that will get your clothes clean.

✠

Very hot water kills germs; cooler water does not. If someone in your family has the flu or other communicable disease, wash their things in very hot water or use a laundry disinfectant.

✠

Don't overload the washer. Overloading reduces the cleaning action, causing more abrasion, more lint and more wrinkles. Too large a load can also waste current by making it necessary for you to wash some of the items over again.

✠

If you have a soak cycle on your washer, use it for heavily soiled items so that you will have to wash them only once. If your washer does not have a soak cycle, lift the lid. The soak period should be relatively short (5-15 minutes) to prevent the redepositing of soil on the clothes.

✠

Soaking in cold water removes many stains—especially those of protein foods, blood, and perspiration.

☥

Don't give clothes too long a washing time. Cottons and linens—even heavily-soiled ones—should not be washed longer than ten minutes or the soil may be redeposited on them. Five minutes is usually enough for synthetics and one to three minutes for woolens.

☥

If your washer has a suds-return feature, you can save hot or warm water for later loads.

☥

Follow detergent instructions carefully. Oversudsing makes a washing machine motor work harder than it needs to.

☥

You can save energy by doing your laundry at home. Washing clothes at home requires only one-third as much energy as making a two-mile round trip by auto and doing them at the laundromat.

☥

Use a non-polluting laundry detergent. If you've ever stood on a bluff above a dam on one of our country's great rivers and watched the detergent foam rising up in great drifts, you'll know why.

☥

If the faucets that serve your washer are where you can reach them, turn them off after you've finished washing for the day. This prevents all that water pressure from beating continually on the inside workings and can sometimes double the life span of a washer.

☥

Avoid using extension cords for washers, dryers, and other major appliances. They're not heavy enough to do the job.

> Be not conformed to this world, but be transformed by the renewing of your mind.
>
> Paul

DRYING

Whenever possible, hang your clothes up instead of using the dryer. Hanging them outdoors can give them that wonderful smell of fresh air.

Hanging clothes indoors or outdoors uses less fuel than running them through a dryer but it does use some. The Energy Research Group at the University of Illinois has computed that roughly 200,000 British Thermal Units of energy are consumed per year in manufacturing, transporting, and selling the necessary clotheslines, clothespins, and clothesline stanchions to hang your wash up. This costs you about $3.40. A gas dryer, however, uses 8,100,000 BTU's annually and an electric dryer 14,000,000—forty to seventy times as much as hanging clothes on a line. Notice that gas dryers use considerably less energy than electric dryers.

The Illinois ERG also has figured that if every owner of an electric clothes dryer went back to hanging the wash to dry in the basement or back yard, enough electricity would be conserved to fill the complete needs of 3.2 million homes.

If you must use a dryer, don't put blankets or rugs in; they take a long time and use a lot of fuel and can so easily be thrown over a fence or bench in the back yard if you don't have clotheslines—or even laid on the ground. Indoors they can be spread over the edge of the laundry tubs or bathtub or over the shower curtain rod. This can add welcome moisture to the house in the winter. Rugs with a rubber backing should not be dried in a dryer anyway.

Use the appropriate dryer setting for each type of fabric. The lower the temperature, the less energy consumed. Permanent-press items can use a warm rather than a hot setting.

Usually whatever you wash together can be dried together. But avoid drying lightweight things with heavy things: don't dry a sheer blouse with bath towels; the blouse could become overdried and wrinkled by the time the towels were done.

Some knit things such as boys' tee shirts can be placed on a hanger when they come out of the washer and hung up to dry. This not only saves fuel but prevents their shrinking, which is sometimes hard to avoid in a dryer.

Pleated skirts should be drip-dried to preserve the pleats.

It doesn't take much time to toss large bath towels over a line in the basement and humidify the winter-dry house while you're saving energy and money. String up a line today so it'll be there the next time you do the laundry.

How about a line for outdoors, too.

Lingerie with elastic will stay new much longer if it isn't put into the dryer. Instead spread it out on the warm top of the dryer.

During the summer, vent your electric dryer outdoors to get rid of the hot, wet air. During the heating season you may want to vent it indoors to make use of this heat and humidity. Unfasten the flexible piping from the wall and place a nylon stocking over the end to catch any lint particles that might get through the filter. The opening in the wall can be stopped up by fitting a piece of metal over the end.

Remove no-iron items from the dryer as soon as they're dry; don't give them a chance to settle and acquire wrinkles.

Dry sheer fabrics such as dacron curtains just after you've dried another load; set the controls for AIR ONLY and use the retained heat.

Damp-drying saves energy and is the easiest way to prepare clothes for ironing without having to sprinkle them. If your dryer doesn't have a damp-dry setting, use a shorter drying time or remove clothes from the dryer before the end of the regular cycle.

Natural fibers such as cotton, silk, and wool need to retain a certain amount of moisture. If they're overdried, they tend to wrinkle and may be hard to iron.

Sometimes you can dry small items in the stored heat from a previous load.

☩

Clean the lint filter of your dryer after every load. Lint collecting on the filter reduces the dryer's efficiency.

✠

When you're installing a new clothes dryer, try to place it in a warm area of your home. In an unheated garage or utility area the dryer will have to run longer to do the same job.

☩

Avoid overloading the dryer. This slows the drying time and can cause wrinkles.

☩

Be sure to follow the instructions of the manufacturer of the garment when you wash or dry it. If only they would all put instructions on the label!

✠

Occasionally wipe the inside of the dryer with a damp cloth to remove any lint that's accumulated.

✠

Several times a year check the vent to make sure it's clear. A clogged vent can prevent the smooth flow of air and lengthen the drying time.

✠

Check the vent on the outside of the house, too.

> He is the best dressed whose dress no one observes.
> Trollope

IRONING

Each warm-up of the iron consumes energy, so try to do your ironing all at once instead of in many small batches.

✠

Many clothes need no ironing if they're removed promptly from the dryer and smoothed out by hand or hung up. Shirts sometimes need to have their fronts pulled into shape a little. Sheets and other flat items can be removed from the dryer before they're fully dry, folded smoothly, and placed on the warm top of the dryer to finish drying.

✠

Begin ironing with fabrics that need the lowest ironing temperature—synthetics, for instance. Move on to the medium temperature for silk and wool, then to the high temperatures for cotton and linen. This reduces warm-up time and makes use of the fact that many irons tend to get a little hotter as they go along.

✠

Be sure to use the correct setting for each fabric to prevent scorching or underpressing.

✠

Use the lowest setting that will do the job well.

✠

Often you can turn the iron off early and finish your pressing on stored heat.

✠

If the phone rings or someone stops in while you're ironing, turn the iron off (unless you're going to continue ironing while you visit) and conserve energy.

✠

An ironing board cover that reflects heat back can speed up ironing time and save electricity.

✠

Many things can be ironed double (two thicknesses at a time), cutting ironing time in two.

✠

Look for clothes that need no ironing when you shop. Even handkerchiefs are available now in permanent press.

�֎

Many people no longer iron dish towels, guest towels, sheets, and pillowcases—these can all be purchased in no-iron fabrics. Even some very attractive tablecloths and napkins come in materials that never need ironing. And place mats come in a variety of materials that need only be sudsed, rinsed, and spread out to dry.

● ● ●

If only I may grow: firmer, simpler—quieter, warmer.
Dag Hammarskjöld

DRYCLEANING

Self-service drycleaning is a very economical way of keeping the family's clothes looking their best. You can drop your clothes in, do your shopping in nearby stores, and pick up the freshly-cleaned clothes when you're ready to go home.

If there's any drycleaning smell when you put the clothes into the car, leave a window or two open so you won't become sleepy. And hang them on an outside clothesline or in the garage until the smell is gone before taking them into the house. The chemicals can be very unhealthy.

Don't allow sleeping bags that've been cleaned to be slept in until all the cleaning smell is gone. The fumes can be fatal.

Many women dryclean their best summer dresses and find that they keep their new look much longer. With self-service drycleaning, the cost is not prohibitive, and they don't need ironing as they might if they had been washed.

Most self-service drycleaning machines take an eight-pound load, but it's not necessary to wait till you have that much of one color. As long as the colors are fast, garments of many colors can be safely drycleaned together.

As soon as the machine shuts off, remove the garments and hang them up to prevent wrinkling.

Items containing plastic, fur, rubber, or leather should not be put in the self-service machines.

If you overload the machine, it's harder for the clothes to dry, and the drycleaning smell is more apt to linger.

Some buttons will melt if they get up against the hot metal in the dryer, so turn items with buttons inside out or cover the buttons loosely with aluminum foil.

Be sure to turn sweaters and other knit garments inside out to prevent the fibers on the outer surface from rubbing against other garments and forming nubby little lumps.

Beware of all enterprises that require new clothes.
Thoreau

MENDING

Mending is one of the most important household arts. To take something that is not wearable and make it wearable—this says love. A mother patching the knees of her child's jeans, a father taking heavy thread and sewing the buckle back on his child's shoes—these say, "We care about you."

Anyone can throw away a dress that gets a rip in a seam or a pair of mittens with a hole in the thumb. Anyone can go out and buy, buy, buy. But the loving, concerned person will mend what he already has—and have something left to give to those in greater need.

✠

If a good wool suit or dress gets a hole, threads from the fabric can often be taken from a seam inside the garment and worked in to fill the hole, matching stitches to the weave of the cloth.

✠

Elbow patches can give a second life to sports coats, sweaters, and jackets. Available at many stores, they can be sewed on either by hand or machine. And when the garment finally wears out, the patches can sometimes be saved and used again.

✟

Iron-on patches for jeans and other garments can save busy mothers a lot of time. Softer patches are also available in a variety of colors for stockings. With a good supply of both the heavy and the softer patches, you should be able to mend almost any item of clothing in moments. And if the patches come loose, they can easily be ironed down again.

✟

If you iron patches on the *inside* of the knees of your children's new jeans, the double thickness will make the knees very long-wearing and you won't have to put a patch on the outside where it would show.

✟

Sew on buttons more strongly *before* they fall off and get lost. Some people routinely sew the buttons on more securely on all the clothes they buy.

✠

If you want to be super-saving, you can take needle and thread and reinforce the heels of new stockings before someone wears them. If you do this in the evening while you're watching TV or listening to the radio, it's as pleasant as doing embroidery.

✠

When you buy a new garment, check it for any places that may need a few stitches to strengthen them. A stitch in time can easily save nine.

✠

Sometimes a small applique can be sewn over a hole in clothing. Teenagers do this with their jeans to extend their usefulness and make them more individual. Or in some cases a decorative pin can cover a small hole. With a little ingenuity you can keep from discarding many items of clothing that are otherwise in good condition.

✙

It's not hard to sew a new zipper in a jacket. This often can be done fairly quickly with a large needle and heavy thread. Or use the sewing machine if you prefer.

✙

New wristlets can give an otherwise good jacket with worn-out cuffs a new lease on life. Added to a child's jacket that didn't have them before and whose sleeves have become a little short, they can give an additional year's wear.

✙

Have you discovered heavy thread? The regular 40, 50, and 60 are good for general sewing, but when it comes to sewing buttons on coats and suits and sewing up jeans and jackets and other heavy things, the heavier threads get the job done more quickly and they last much longer. Look for button and carpet thread or heavy duty thread.

✠

A man's suit or overcoat, which is often a major family investment, can have its life extended in various ways. Worn pockets can be sewn up, have iron-on patches applied, or have new pockets (obtainable at notions counters or you can make your own) sewn in.

✠

Frayed buttonholes can be reworked with button and carpet thread and loose buttons sewn on more securely.

✠

When the front edges of a man's suit or coat begin to show wear, get matching thread and cover the weak spots with small hand stitching.

✠

When the cuffs on the sleeves of a man's suit or coat begin to fray, poke the edge inward—that is, don't fold it over to the inside of the sleeve, but tuck the edge down inside itself so it disappears. Then, taking small blind stitches that don't show, sew up the new edge. Since the cuffs are usually the first thing to wear out on a coat or suit, this can sometimes double the life of the garment.

✠

Invest in shoe polish for each color of shoes you own. Many shoes that look ready for the discard pile only need a good coat of polish.

✠

If the handle on a good purse wears out, take it to your shoe repair shop, which should either have replacement handles or by-the-yard leather handle material.

✠

Look into the other things the shoe shop can do for your family besides sewing up ripped shoes, replacing soles and heels, and repairing shoe linings. They can also work on many other leather items—belts, notebooks, jackets, gloves, briefcases, luggage.

✛

If the dog chews the heel off a woman's shoe, the shoe shop has replacement heels in various styles and colors.

✛

Sometimes a pair of shoes will stretch until they're too loose to wear. Pick up a pair of cushiony inner soles at the shoe shop or department store and your shoes will not only fit better but be more comfortable. There are also pads made for under the tongue of the shoe and for the back of the heel that can help create a better fit.

✠

If you have a pair of shoes that fit well and are comfortable and you still like the style, they're worth repairing.

✠

Make it a rule to never throw away good clothing. Exchange children's outgrown clothing with friends or give it to a church or community group.

Coats and suits that are too worn to be usable can be made into warm quilts for people in needy areas. Never throw out a warm coat or suit.

Clothing is a necessity that is in short supply in some parts of the world. Use yours wisely and pass it along when you've finished with it.

• • •

And why are you anxious about clothing?
Jesus

Cooking and Baking

Grandma had a saying when it came to food: "waste not, want not."
Instead of throwing away the green leaves of the celery, she used them
to flavor soups and stews. She cooked up a kettle of nourishing corn-
meal, cream of wheat, or oatmeal for her family's breakfast, then
packed what was left into a loaf tin and sliced and fried it for the
next morning's breakfast.

She saved dry bread to make a savory dressing for a roast chicken.
And at the end of each week she made a hearty soup to use up all the
week's vegetables.

There are many ways of using up leftover foods, helping the world's
food supply as well as helping the family's budget. There are also ways
of cooking and baking that can save fuel—and dollars.

Many vegetables are delicious raw. You can serve these and other
vegetables alone, with a dip or in a salad—broccoli, cauliflower, cabbage, carrots, spinach, celery, tomatoes.

✠

Serving your family fresh fruits instead of pies and other pastries for
dessert gives them better nourishment, saves you work and conserves
fuel.

LEFTOVERS

Many leftover foods taste better if they're not reheated. Beef, pork, chicken, and turkey make excellent sandwiches or additions to salads or fruit plates. Leftover broccoli, asparagus, beans, and other vegetables can be added to salads or vegetable plates.

✛

Leftover meats or fish can also be used in casseroles, soups, stews, and as a flavoring for cooked vegetables.

✛

Bread that has gotten a little dry can also be used in French toast, Apple Betty, old-fashioned bread pudding, or a crumb topping for casseroles.

✠

Leftover rice can be combined with ground meat and seasonings for meat balls, croquettes, or stuffed peppers. Or the rice can be mixed with tiny marshmallows, crushed pineapple, and whipped cream for a delicious dessert.

�֎

Egg whites can be used in meringues, frostings, divinity, tortes, white cakes; egg yolks in homemade noodles, frostings, cooked salad dressings, and Hollandaise sauce. A few whites or yolks can be added to whole eggs to make scrambled eggs.

> Every man should eat and drink, and enjoy the good of all his labors, it is the gift of God.
>
> Ecclesiastes

COOKING

If you use an electric stove, shut off the burner a minute or two before the food has finished cooking and let it finish cooking on the accumulated heat.

✛

Cover kettles whenever possible with a tight-fitting lid to keep the heat in. You'll be able to use a lower setting, and food will cook faster.

✛

Place kettles on the burner before you turn the heat on to save fuel.

✠

By using ceramic or glass kettles you can lower the temperature as much as 25 degrees.

✠

Cooking with as little water as possible conserves energy as well as preserving the nutritive value of the food. Use 2-4 tablespoons of water for packaged frozen vegetables and 1/3 to 1/2 cup of water for fresh vegetables. Some fresh foods that are high in moisture—tomatoes, spinach, apples, and rhubarb—can be cooked without water.

✠

A plastic pouch of vegetables can be placed in a kettle of cooking potatoes, eliminating one burner.

✠

Frozen vegetables and meats that are thawed to room temperature first require less heat to cook. A frozen roast requires one-third more energy to cook than a thawed one.

✠

Since water can get no hotter than 212° F., there is no need to have a burner on any higher than what will just barely keep the water boiling.

✠

If you're cooking with kettles of heavy aluminum, heat the pan until the lid is too hot to touch, then turn the burner down to a lower setting. Whatever kind of cookware you're using, turn down the burner to a lower setting once the food reaches the boiling point.

✠

You can save fuel in cooking noodles and macaroni by dropping them in a kettle of rapidly boiling water, bringing the water back to a boil and cooking them for three minutes, stirring constantly, then turning off the burner, putting on a tight-fitting lid and letting them sit for ten minutes.

✠

Prunes and other dried fruits can be prepared by using almost no fuel. Place them in a glass jar, pour boiling water over them, screw on the lid and place them in the refrigerator when they're cool. They'll be ready to eat the next morning.

✠

Some foods like frankfurters can be cooked by placing them in a pan of boiling water, removing the pan from the heat, covering it and allowing it to stand for 8 to 10 minutes.

✠

Use the size kettle that fits the burner. Too small a kettle will let heat escape around it; too large a kettle can cause the stove top around the burner to be damaged by the heat of the pan. Kettles should not extend more than one inch beyond the edge of the burner.

Be sure the bottoms of kettles are flat so that they will establish firm contact with the burner. An aluminum pan that has warped can be made flat again by turning it upside down, placing a large wooden block over the warped area and pounding the block with a hammer.

Thermostatically controlled surface units with a heat-sensing element in the center save energy by cycling on and off.

Heating water in a tea kettle uses less energy than heating it in a pan.

Make sure all burners are turned off when you've finished using them.

Using the exhaust fan above the stove can draw off heat and make the house cooler in the summer. But in the winter it should be used more briefly to avoid sending too much of the house's heat up the flue.

If your range has a food warmer, you may find it more economical than the oven or surface units for keeping foods heated.

A pressure cooker makes sense for certain dishes because steam speeds up the cooking process.

If you're using a gas stove, take a good look at the flame. If the burner is operating properly, it'll be a clear blue. If there are traces of yellow, the burner holes may have become clogged with food particles and should be cleaned. Lift off the burners and clean the ports with a wire pipe cleaner (never use a toothpick). If the yellow persists, call the appliance serviceman to make an adjustment. Keeping the flame blue will improve the efficiency of the range and save you money.

 Eat to live: live not to eat.
Benjamin Franklin

BAKING

When you're placing several pans in the oven and using both racks, be sure there's space around each pan so that things will bake evenly. Stagger the pans so that no pan is squarely above the other. Also leave space between the pans on each shelf and space the racks so that there's 1½ inches of air space above and below each pan.

✠

If you must open the oven while it's on, make it as brief as possible; an oven can take up to ten minutes to reach its temperature again after it's been open a long time. It's better to use an automatic timer, meat thermometer, and see-through glass window to check on the progress of whatever you're baking.

✠

If you want to make only a few things—a few potatoes or apples or a small cake—and if you have very heavy aluminum cookware, you can do it on the stove. Place the food in a kettle, covering it tightly, and keep the burner on high until the lid becomes too hot to touch, then turn it down to a very low setting. This can save a lot of fuel.

✠

Plan to bake several things if you're going to be running the oven anyway. If you're doing a roast or casserole, slip in some potatoes, squash, corn meal muffins, banana bread, or an apple crisp.

✠

If you're cooking several dishes at once and they require slightly different temperatures (say 325, 350 and 375), pick the mean temperature (350) to cook all three and remove each one as it's done.

✠

The temperature is higher at the top of the oven, so put the foods that need the higher temperature on the top rack.

✠

Using the oven can be less expensive than using the stove if you bake enough items at once. Most surface units stay on the whole time they're in use, but an oven is on a while, off a while, with the insulation holding the heat in in between.

✠

Quantity baking can help you save fuel. Instead of baking just one loaf of bread, bake several and freeze the extras.

✠

When you're preheating the oven, do not set the thermostat higher than the required temperature. There's nothing to be gained by dialing a higher setting because the oven won't heat any faster.

✠

Preheating the oven is often unnecessary. Generally any food requiring more than a full hour of baking time may be placed in a cold oven to use the heat as soon as it begins.

✠

You can warm plates and foods in an oven that's been used and recently turned off.

❀

Since glass and ceramic dishes transfer heat better than metal, you can lower the oven setting 25 degrees when you're baking in them.

BROILING

Broilers require no preheating, thereby conserving energy.

✠

With proper planning, a complete meal can be prepared at once under the broiler.

✠

The broiler can be turned off shortly before the food is done and the food will finish cooking on the stored heat.

APPLIANCES

For specialized jobs, small appliances can use less electricity than a range. It costs three times as much to toast bread in an oven as in a pop-up toaster. Also among the fuel-savers are electric skillets, popcorn poppers, electric grills, portable ovens and broilers, and electric fondue and bean pots.

✠

Some portable appliances also double as serving dishes. By cutting down on the number of dishes that need to be washed, they save on hot water and dishwasher loads.

✠

Keep all portable cooking appliances out of drafts. Cool air circulating around them can reduce their efficiency.

✠

You can prepare several foods at once in an electric skillet by dividing it with inserts of aluminum foil.

Family Fun

Back in the days before tv, radio, movies, jet travel, ski resorts, power boats, and automobiles, grandpa and grandma had a lot of fun anyway. They had parties and picnics and get-togethers, taffy pulls and wiener roasts and square dances, hayrides through the country-side, horseback rides through the woods, raft rides down the river, quilting bees, spelling bees, barn-raising bees, hay-mowing bees. And walks down a country lane smelling the falling leaves in the autumn and the newly-turned earth in the spring.

They must have had as much fun as we do today—maybe more.

And they caused less pollution to the world around them.

Going somewhere on a fast jet can be exciting—but some of the excitement is lost when jet exhaust nearly asphyxiates you as you walk from your car to the plane you're to board.

Speeding over the water in a sleek boat can be exhilarating—until you look behind at the blue pall you've cast over the lake.

Driving 1500 miles to a ski slope to imprint a double track down the mountainside can be thrilling—but not to the people along your 1500-mile route who must breathe the carbon monoxide you've left in your wake.

Skimming over powdery drifts in the park in a snowmobile can be envigorating—but not to the hikers driven out by the noise and fumes you make.

There are many ways of having fun that add little or no pollution—

toboganning, sledding, skating, snowshoeing, and skiing nearer home, swimming, surfing, snorkeling, tennis, badminton, golf.

And what ever happened to propelling a boat under one's own power? Bigger is not necessarily better—in boats as in many other things. Canoeing, rowing, and sailing can be better for us and for the environment.

✠

Hiking can put roses in your cheeks—and you can gain a new closeness to nature. When was the last time you watched a bird build a nest? A rabbit scamper across the meadow? A squirrel chase a friend (his, not yours) up a tree?

✠

How long has it been since your family went bicycling? Roller skating? Played volley ball? Built a snowman? Had a game of croquet?

✠

For indoor activity how about Ping-Pong, darts, pool, Carroms, Twister. There's an indoor sport providing the kind of exercise each person needs.

✠

Every year there are more games on the market, some based on chance, some on skill, and most on a combination of these. Some are designed so that even very young family members can play at their own level of ability with the rest of the family.

✠

Have a card table handy for spreading out the pieces of a big jig-saw puzzle—family members can stop and find places for a few pieces whenever they pass it.

✠

When you get tired of the puzzles you have, trade off with friends for a while, picking friends who'll agree to check and see that every piece is there before putting the puzzle back in the box.

✠

The day breaks and makes all things alive,
joyous, happy, full of activity.

Martin Luther

Some families play word games at meals. Someone says a letter, for instance. The next person must, by adding one letter, create a word. Each person in turn must do the same. (The letters can be mixed around into a different order.) Whenever a person can't add a letter to form a new word, he must put one of his pieces of silverware into a central location—possibly an empty serving dish. When a player has lost all the silverware he can afford to lose (and still go on eating), he's out of the game. The last person still in the game wins.

✠

Other families like rhyming games. The first person says, "Today I saw . . ." then adds an adjective and a noun: "a friendly beagle." The next person might say, "a bald eagle" and the next, "a moth-eaten sea gull" (you can stretch the rhyming a little). Whoever can't think of a rhyming set of words gets skipped, and the next person gets to start a new set of words.

✠

Some families like to read minute-mysteries aloud and see who can guess who did it.

✠

Others enjoy "Existential Botticelli." The person who is "it" thinks of some well-known person and gives the first letter of his or her last name—B, for instance. Another player then might ask, "Are you a famous composer and conductor?" "It" must then think of someone whose name starts with B who fits that description; he might say, "No, I am not Leonard Bernstein." (The one who asks must have someone in mind who fits the description.) If "it" can't come up with a suitable name, the one who asked may ask a question that calls for a Yes or No answer such as "Are you a woman?" or "Are you a musician?"

✠

Even a not-too-musically-talented family can have fun singing around the piano or organ. Or getting together with whatever instruments family members play. Or improvising with bells, a rubber-bands-on-a-cardboard-box violin, glasses filled to various levels with water, oatmeal boxes with spoons for drumsticks—whatever you happen to have around the house.

✠

The recorder is an instrument that is inexpensive, has a beautiful tone, and can be learned in a short time.

✠

Some families have returned to some of the old-time instruments—zithers, dulcimers, theorbos, mandolins. The sounds are lovely and different.

✠

Some instruments can be built from kits—organs, harpsichords, clavichords, dulcimers, and others. This can be a good project for some families.

✠

Stereo and radio can bring the world's finest music into your home; and despite its many inferior, infuriating programs, TV does offer some good things. Enjoy. But remember that a color TV set uses nearly nine times as much energy as a radio. You may want to turn the TV off and the radio on if you'll only be listening, not watching.

✠

If no one's watching the TV or listening to the radio, it's usually best to turn them off and conserve electricity. But if a TV is continually turned off and on, the repeated heating and cooling of the tubes will wear them out sooner. So if there's only a short interval between the things you want to watch, it may be better to leave it on.

✠

If you have an instant-on TV, unplug it when it won't be in use for an extended time—while you're on vacation, for instance.

✠

Toys are an important part of family life. Children need toys that are safe and suited to their age, abilities, and interests. Toys that allow the child to use his imagination—blocks, for instance—are better than those that do everything for him. With a large enough supply of blocks of many sizes, a child can create an endless variety of things. The blocks can be either purchased at a store or homemade; you can get scrap lumber at the lumber yard and saw it to various sizes, sanding off the rough edges. Children can start playing with blocks at a very early age and continue enjoying them for many years.

✠

Tinker Toys are another toy that has appeal for many ages. Grade-schoolers like them, junior high kids—and in some college dorms students each buy a box and put them all together to create something super colossal.

✠

Try to avoid toys that need batteries; replacing them becomes so expensive that eventually the toy is put on the shelf and forgotten. And any toy that depends on what *it* does rather than on what the *child* does is going to become boring pretty fast anyway.

✢

Things you already have around the house often make the best toys. Little girls (little boys, too) can be given a low shelf in a kitchen cupboard for their very own—with a few of mother's extra things such as an individual jello mold, a plastic scraper, a pastry brush, a tiny kettle. When mother empties a small box (such as a pudding or jello box), it can become part of the child's treasured wares.

✠

If a boy (or a girl) has a hammer and a saw his size plus some scrap lumber and nails, he can build all kinds of things.

✠

Avoid giving children brittle plastic toys that will soon break. These toys can be a great disappointment and give them a frightening idea of the world—that nothing is permanent and they dare not learn to like anything because it's just going to break anyway.

✢

The more a toy leaves to the child's imagination, the better; the best toys are those that provide the stuff from which a child can create things. A container of beads and a package of wire plus some suggested designs for making a ring are better than six plastic pieces that need only to be snapped together.

✠

Modeling clay can be made easily and inexpensively at home. Combine 2½ cups of flour and ½ cup of salt. Dissolve 1 tablespoon of powdered alum (this keeps the clay fresh) in 2 cups of boiling water. Mix all the ingredients, then add 3 tablespoons of corn oil and blend. You can add a little food coloring if you want, but this can sometimes come off on clothes.

✢

A box of crayons, package of pipe cleaners, odds and ends of yarn, box of watercolor paints, and stack of paper can give a child many hours of fun. Some families have a "make-it" box in which they keep all the things that can be used for art projects.

✢

Small children need soft, cuddly things. A doll made from a sock, simple and huggable, is much more enjoyable for a small child than a hard doll meticulously dressed in the costume of some particular country or period.

Good toys should do one or more of these things:

help the child have fun,
help him understand the world around him,
further his muscular development,
help him develop skills,
help him relate well to other children,
encourage him to be creative,
give him practice in reasoning and imagination,
let him explore the arts and sciences,
let him explore hobbies and careers.

Cardboard boxes can be made into all sorts of toys. Turn one upside down, draw burners and control knobs on the top, an oven, broiler, and kettle drawer on the front, and you have a stove. Draw a lid and control knobs on the top of another box, cut around the lid on three sides so it opens, and you have an automatic washer. Or make a refrigerator, freezer, or other appliance.

Cardboard boxes can also be cut to make a child's table and chairs. Follow the design of those in the toy section of a catalog.

A box of costumes and old clothes can give children a lot of fun. You don't need to buy new costumes for this—put in some of mom's and dad's discarded clothes. Pick up a few interesting things at the next rummage sale, adding interesting old hats, jewelry, shoes, scarves, gloves, belts.

You can make costumes for preschoolers from old pillow cases. Cut a head hole in the sewn-up end and arm holes along the side edges. Then the child, using crayons, can color on black stripes (if it's a white pillow case) to make it a zebra, black spots on a yellow case to make a leopard, brown spots on a green case to make a frog—or whatever strikes his fancy. An appropriate mask will add to the fun.

Set aside areas in your home for hobbies—a workbench for woodworking, perhaps a special one for the jewelry makers in the family and another for those who like to work with electronics—or for any other hobbies your family may have. Workbenches can be put together very inexpensively from old lumber, unused tables and stands, etc., etc.

✠

Many crafts utilize things that would otherwise be thrown away: small pieces of cloth can be made into doll clothes, outworn woolen clothing into hooked rugs, nut shells into wreaths or amusing little characters, tin cans into candleholders. Someone somewhere can usually find a good use for the things other people throw away.

✠

Some families make their own Christmas tree ornaments from used thread spools, pieces of egg cartons, pine cones, costume jewelry, bits of cloth, cardboard, ribbon, paper, glitter, sequins, lace, velvet. This can give children a good project while they wait for Christmas.

✠

If you can find stones in your yard or when you go for walks, you can turn them into interesting creatures. Glue a small one on top of a larger one, paint a kitty face and whiskers on the upper one and a tail and paws on the lower one. Or stack up three sizes of white stones, glue them together, and paint on the face and buttons of a snowman. Or glue three stones onto a branch and paint them to look like owls sitting in a tree.

✠

Libraries usually have a good collection of books on crafts if you need more ideas.

✠

If you'd like to help your family develop its creative thinking, whenever a suitable situation arises you might try asking one or more of these four questions:

1. What else could we do with this?
2. What could we use instead of this?
3. How else could we do this?
4. What would happen if we . . . ?

✠

Display things made by family members around the house.

✠

A collection of keys, bells, campaign buttons—or whatever else a family member collects—can be mounted on burlap, velvet, cotton, or some other fabric, then framed and hung on the wall.

Hang up the things that are most meaningful to your family—pictures of your children, brothers and sisters, parents, grandparents, great-grandparents. One family uses a long hall as their family gallery—fun for the family and for visitors.

Some families hang up certificates family members have received—school diplomas, life-saving course certificates, beekeeping licenses, safe driving awards.

If you have things made by grandparents or great-grandparents—grandpa's woodworking, grandma's embroidered pictures—hang them or place them where the family can enjoy them. This can give children a sense of being part of the human family and of a particular family.

If we can't drive our cars as much, perhaps we'll have a chance to enjoy the members of our family more.

Perhaps we'll have more time to have neighbors and friends in for picnics in the back yard, for popcorn, for singing Christmas carols.

Perhaps we'll have more time for reading and for thinking and for getting to know ourselves.

Perhaps we'll have time to take more notice of nature around us. We'll notice that the new buds are already there on the bare trees in the fall, that the caterpillars have warmer coats this winter, that the neighborhood has more crocuses and daffodils this spring.

The government can never ration the basic pleasures. Family, friends, and the world of nature around us—these are lasting sources of pleasure. Perhaps now we will enjoy them more than we ever have.

We are growing serious and, let me tell you, that's the very next step to being dull.

Addison

Gardening

Grandma took pride in the big meaty tomatoes she grew in her garden. When she peeled them and sliced them and arranged them, bright red and juicy, on a plate, they were almost a meal in themselves.

Her green beans, freshly picked, were so tender that they were almost a different food from those she would have purchased in the store.

And her pot of chives on the kitchen windowsill with their piquant onion flavor made her creamed potatoes, vegetable salads, and beef soup legendary.

Those who garden say that nothing in all the world makes a person feel as close to nature and to God as working up the soil, planting the seeds, tending the young plants and finally carrying in the wonderful, colorful harvest—the red radishes, beets, tomatoes, and rhubarb; the orange carrots, peppers, and pumpkins; the yellow squash, beans, and corn; the green leaf lettuce, cabbage, okra, peas, cucumber, broccoli, Swiss chard, spinach and watermelons; the brown potatoes, cantaloupes, and onions; and the purple eggplant.

Gardens can also be a good therapy. It's hard to feel nervous in a row of carrots. And the cares that a person brings with him to the garden somehow seem to unravel as he digs away at the earth's surface; when he takes a hoe in hand, worries and fears seem to fall away.

GARDENING IN CONTAINERS

Not everyone, unfortunately, has room for a full-scale garden. With more and more people living in apartments each year, fewer and fewer families have a piece of ground to spade up; but there are other ways. Many food plants can be grown outdoors in containers on apartment balconies, on terraces, doorsteps, window ledges, and in window boxes. And apartment dwellers, because they are almost completely cut off from the soil, sometimes become the most enthusiastic gardeners of all.

What kinds of food plants can be grown in containers? Green beans, radishes, Swiss chard, tomatoes, peppers, leaf lettuce, rhubarb, cabbage, chives, and onions all do well in large pots.

Cucumbers and summer squash can be planted in pots atop a wall. They need a lot of room for vines and will look very attractive cascading over the ledge.

Tomatoes probably offer the largest return for your time and effort if you have a sunny spot. They do well in containers, and cherry tomato plants can be trimmed down a little and brought inside when cold weather comes. Kept in a sunny window, they'll provide a display of blossoms and ripening fruit as well as tomatoes for the family table all through the winter.

You may already have containers that you can use for minigardens: plastic or clay pots, concrete urns, old pails, jardinieres, barrels, plastic buckets, bushel baskets, wire baskets, or wooden boxes. Almost any container is satisfactory, from tiny pots for your window ledges to large wooden boxes for your patio.

Plastic laundry baskets that have many open spaces in their design can be lined with plastic sheeting to hold the soil. If your containers have no holes, you can drill some on the sides near the bottom (but not on the bottom). Wood containers such as bushel baskets will last up to five years if they're painted inside and out with a safe wood preservative.

If you have no suitable containers, they're readily available in garden stores. Some very attractive ones are made from fiberglass, metal alloys, glazed ceramics, or textured concrete.

But keep in mind that clay pots, because they're porous and permit the passage of air and moisture, are the most natural and therefore the easiest containers to grow things in. Many knowledgeable gardeners won't plant in anything else.

Be sure to consider the amount of outdoor sunlight you have. If you have a good supply of sun, you can grow fruiting plants such as tomatoes, peppers, and cucumbers. Root vegetables such as carrots, beets, and radishes can get along with a little less sun, and leafy vegetables (lettuce, cabbage, greens of all kinds) can stand more shade yet.

If you train or arrange your plants vertically on stakes, trellises, or fences, you can make better use of the sunlight you have—and of the ground space.

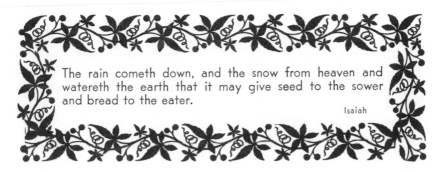

The rain cometh down, and the snow from heaven and watereth the earth that it may give seed to the sower and bread to the eater.

Isaiah

INDOOR GARDENING

You might enjoy growing your own herbs. Many herbs do well in pots and make an attractive display indoors or out—and give that added special touch to your favorite dishes. Parsley and chives can be brought indoors in the fall to a sunny window, as can many other interesting little plants that offer fragrance and flavor.

Houseplants of all kinds add oxygen to the air and bring a little of nature indoors, adding to the joy of living. You might want to try some narcissus or amaryllis bulbs for winter blossoms. Their dramatic bursts of bloom remind us that, despite winter's icy blasts, spring will come again.

But remember that the higher the temperature in the room, the more sun and water your plants will have to have. A shortage of fuel and cooler rooms suit houseplants just fine.

It's also possible to grow bean sprouts in your kitchen. For about one-fourth the cost of a can of bean sprouts you can produce your own —and this is especially fun for children to watch. The process is very simple.

1. Wash enough soy or mung beans to fill a one- or two-quart jar one-sixth full, removing any broken beans.

2. Cover the beans with at least four times their volume of luke-warm water and let them stand for a few hours, or, at most, overnight, until they are swollen.
3. Pour off the water, rinse the beans with fresh water, drain them and cover the top of the jar with a thin cloth (such as cheese-cloth) and tie it on securely.
4. Place the jar in a dark cupboard and turn it upside down so the water can drain off.
5. Three or four times a day run water in and out of the jar, rinsing away any mold or bacteria that might have developed.
6. In four to six days when the sprouts are 1½ to 2 inches long and before rootlets have formed they are ready to be used in cooking.

The sprouting process gives the beans more vitamin C, a two-fold increase in niacin and a four-fold increase in riboflavin. What other vegetable can you grow at any time of the year, in any climate, in your own kitchen, with nothing but the seed, a jar, and water, that rivals meat in nutritive value, matures in six days or less, requires no sun-shine, creates no waste, can be cooked quickly with just a little fuel, and rivals tomatoes in vitamin C?

• • •

It is not the gardeners and their planting and watering who count, but God, who makes it grow.

Paul

GARDENING IN A SMALL SPACE

If you have even a small yard—and many townhouses and condo-miniums do—you can grow a good assortment of things for your table. In a 12 x 15 foot space you can produce enough tomatoes, leaf lettuce, onions, spinach, broccoli, and carrots to keep a small family sup-plied all during the growing season and even have some to freeze for the winter months.

If your soil is not suitable for gardening, you can consult your garden store dealer or county agent about what to do for it. Often all that's needed is to work in some peat or organic material of some kind to make the soil lighter and more workable.

Or you might want to consider nailing together some boards like a sandbox and having a load of topsoil hauled in to fill it for an instant garden.

You can also use food-giving plants in the plantings around your house. Strawberries make a good low border, and with some varieties each plant can give a quart of delicious fruit. Lettuce, parsley, and other herbs also make interesting taller background plants. Actually almost any vegetable can be mixed in with flowers to add variety and interest. And what's wrong with a strictly edible planting? In many countries the dooryard garden is an integral part of family life, picturesque and practical.

If you have space for a hedge, why not make it raspberry bushes and have a supply of the tasty, otherwise expensive fruit for eating fresh, freezing, and making jam. Grapes can be grown next to the house if you have room for two posts and some wires between them.

FRUIT TREES

Thanks to the new dwarf and semi-dwarf fruit trees, you can now raise apples, peaches, pears, plums, and other fruits in even the smallest yard—some are only three or four feet tall. And they bear fruit at a younger age than full-size trees.

Dwarf trees also have other advantages: they can be sprayed adequately with very inexpensive equipment; they're easier to prune; and they let you have more kinds of trees—you can plant two apple, two peach, two pear and two plum trees in the space that would normally be taken up by one full-size apple tree.

So far apple and pear trees are the best of the dwarf trees. A dwarf apple tree can produce up to four bushels of fruit each year, beginning production the third or fourth year after it's planted. (But don't expect a full crop the first year or so that it produces.) A semi-dwarf tree, the next largest size, can produce up to ten bushels of apples a year. Yellow Delicious trees come into production quickly and produce heavily; Red Delicious take a little longer.

Sweet cherries, if they'll grow in your area, can supply your family with one of the most luscious of fruits plus a lovely display of blossoms in the spring.

71

But don't plant fruit trees unless you plan to give them the care they need. Unless you can encourage a good number of birds to build their nests in your yard and keep down the insect population, you'll have to do a little spraying. Be careful to use only the recommended amount of spray, and do it when there is no wind and when people are not outdoors. Spraying also helps keep fungus, molds, bacteria, and other unwanted things under control, should these become a problem.

It's important too that you don't leave any fruit on the ground to decay. This can spread problems to your own trees and to other trees in the vicinity. Being a good neighbor requires that you keep your trees healthy so that they won't infect those of the people living around you.

Once the fruit begins to ripen on your trees, you may find that your children much prefer it to what you can buy in the store. Some children who routinely choose candy in preference to commercially-distributed fruit suddenly develop a liking for fruit when they taste it from a home orchard. This is probably because commercial growers have tended over the years to work to develop fruit that will ripen quickly, have a good color, and not bruise easily in picking or shipping —and these are not necessarily the qualities that make fruit delicious. But if you grow your own fruit, you won't have to worry about damage from picking and shipping or about having a redder apple than your competitor, so you can order trees that just produce tender, flavorful fruit.

• • •

To every thing there is a season . . . a time to plant, and a time to pluck up that which is planted.

Ecclesiastes

THE COMPOST HEAP

If you're going to garden, you'll certainly want to have a compost heap—a pile of leaves, grass clippings and fruit and vegetable peelings to which you add some natural fertilizer and soil, then let it work for a few months to turn itself into a pile of loose, rich, workable earth.

Many countries have known for centuries that the earth can replenish itself if we give it back the materials to work with, and we all have the natural materials if we'd quit putting them out for the garbage man. In some areas people have taken and taken from the land, never putting anything back, until it's so worn out that all they know how to do is to move on to another place; but with proper care, a piece of land will go on producing well indefinitely.

To create a compost heap all you need is a small piece of ground—even 3 x 3 feet will do. You can enclose the pile with four boards or wire fencing to keep it in place—or not, as you please. Then keep adding anything from your lawn, kitchen, and garden that is decomposable (don't put in sticks, branches or fats). Add some good farm manure or packaged manure from the garden store—or, if you have a dog, turn a problem into an asset.

Turn over the pile occasionally to keep the bacteria working throughout, and add water if it gets too dry. That's all. In a few months you'll have a pile of light, tillable, natural soil to add to your lawn, garden, and flower beds. When you lift out the first rich forkful, you'll probably be hooked for life on gardening.

MULCHING

You'll also want to mulch your garden. Everyone knows that if a piece of ground is dug up, it'll soon have all kinds of weeds growing in it, that the soil will dry out and blow in all directions with the first strong wind, that the rains will do their best to wash the soil away and the sun to dry it out.

The answer to these problems is mulching—spreading a three- to six-inch layer of material over the ground. This material could be grass clippings, sawdust, straw, or compost.

Mulching is probably one of the most valuable things you can do for your garden. Besides holding down weeds, preventing the soil from blowing or washing away, and keeping it moist, cool, and crumbly, mulching also adds valuable organic matter. At the end of the growing season you can work the mulch into the soil to provide organic matter for the following year.

If the sawdust you use for mulching is not well-rotted, you should add one or two cups of ammonium sulfate or sodium nitrate to each bushel before applying it to the garden. Your county agent can give you helpful advice and pamphlets on mulching and on many other aspects of gardening.

You might want to try keeping bees as a hobby. With one hive and a very small amount of work you can produce all the honey your family can eat—and get your fruit trees, flowers, and vegetables pollinated as a fringe benefit. Some people keep bees even in large cities; with proper handling they're no problem to the people around them.

Insofar as possible, in all your gardening use natural rather than artificial aids—natural fertilizers, pesticides, and herbicides; the less we upset nature with unnatural things, the more it can do for us. We must do all we can to maintain the balance of nature—our lives hang in that delicate balance.

Years ago people raised almost all of their food; they ate bountifully and felt close to nature. Those who garden today can do the same.

To dig and delve in nice clean dirt
Can do a mortal little hurt.

J. K. Bangs

ḥealth and ꝑersonal Gare

Long before the days of TV snacks, TV dinners and late, late shows on TV, grandpa and grandma and their family slept eight good hours every night, started the day with a hearty breakfast (the smell of bacon frying brought them all downstairs a little quicker), didn't snack on over-refined foods, and got their exercise and kept their weight down by chopping wood, carrying water in from the pump, milking the cows, gathering eggs, and chasing the chickens out of the garden.

Today health researchers at the University of California at Los Angeles have found that those who follow seven health habits live significantly longer, healthier lives. The seven habits:

1. Getting eight hours of sleep each night
2. Eating breakfast each morning
3. Not eating snack foods
4. Maintaining proper weight
5. Not smoking
6. Drinking only in moderation
7. Getting moderate exercise

After surveying some 7000 Californians and following them for 5½ years, Dr. Lester Breslow and his UCLA associates found that the health of men in their mid-50s who follow six or seven of these good health practices is, on the average, as good as that of men 20 years younger who follow only three or less of them.

They also found that men in the 65 to 74 age-group who've been following them have no higher death rate than men in the 45 to 64 age group who ignore most of them.

"Individual responsibility is a highly important factor in determining good health," Dr. Breslow says.

IMPROVING YOUR OWN HEALTH

Can people of any age improve their health by starting to follow these good health practices? Studies of cigarette smokers show that if a person stops smoking, one year later his chances of dying from coronary heart disease are significantly less. And that ten years after he's quit smoking his risk of lung cancer is no greater than that of a non-smoker.

Dr. Breslow points out that it's often hard to convince young people of the importance of following good health habits because they see people their own age who don't follow them living apparently healthy lives. But after the age of 45 things begin to catch up with them, and the value of good health habits becomes more apparent.

Among the 7000 subjects studied during the 5½ years, deaths among those in the poor habits group (three good habits or less) were 2% for those under 45; 7% for those 45 to 54; 31% for those 55 to 64; 42% for those 65 to 74; and 75% for those over 75. But for those who had followed at least six of the seven health habits, the death rate was only zero, 4%, 9%, 18% and 41%—about half or less.

My soul is dark with stormy riot
Directly traceable to diet.

Hoffenstein

GOOD NUTRITION

Good nutrition is an important part of good health. Food plays a part in three of the seven health habits: breakfast every morning, no snack foods, and keeping a proper weight.

Back in the days before food was so highly processed, when people ate vegetables and fruits and grains fresh from the land, getting all the nourishment one needed was not much of a problem. Not so today. Many of the foods we eat have been so tampered with that we might as well forget trying to get any food value from them.

So what can a person have for breakfast? Some fruit in as natural a state as possible, milk, some grain that's had as little nourishment removed from it as possible, and protein of some sort—eggs, meat, peanut butter, cheese.

Fresh fruit can be expensive, so you might want to consider raising your own or picking it at a pick-your-own orchard, then canning, freezing, or drying it. But there are less expensive foods that can help you get some of the important vitamins during the day. Potatoes and cabbage are good sources of vitamin C—and of many other good things as well. The family that has potatoes once a day will be laying a good foundation for health.

If you serve fruit for dessert instead of baked goods, you'll improve your family's nutrition without stretching your food budget. And the person who eats fruit instead of cake is more apt to feel satisfied and won't soon be looking for something else to snack on. Often it's the person whose body craves proper nourishment who keeps snacking.

And when it comes to proteins, there are many good sources besides pork and beef—sources that are considerably less expensive. Eggs, fish, cheese, and chicken are all good buys. So are beans, peas, and nuts. Both soybeans and peanuts have complete proteins and therefore can replace meat in every essential way.

Nutritionists have found that if you really need an inexpensive source of protein, it's hard to beat a peanut butter sandwich. Health food stores have delicious peanut butter made without hydrogenated fats, sugar, salt, or preservatives—just good, fresh peanuts smoothed to a creamy butter.

Have you discovered soybeans? Soybeans contain twice the available protein of beef—and twice the iron. They have 23 times as much vitamin B as beef and 26 times as much calcium. Yet they have none of the cholesterol beef has—rather they are rich in *cholesterol-reducing* substances.

Native to China, soybeans have been the most important source of food there for almost 4500 years, furnishing almost the sole source of protein for the whole country. Though soybeans are now the number one cash crop in the U.S., we have only begun to discover the delicious, inexpensive, nourishing dishes that can be made from them.

And the farmer can produce one pound of soybeans or other legumes or grains much more inexpensively than he can a pound of meat—which we can all be thankful for with high meat prices.

Many families use non-fat dry milk to help keep down food costs. Some mix it with water according to directions, then add it to fresh milk, one to one, for drinking; others drink it without the addition of fresh milk. It can be used in making puddings, baked goods, and many other good things. Add a little powdered milk wherever you can for extra nutrition.

Cereals and grains can pose a problem now that many are so refined that cardboard would be almost as nourishing. Cereals that you cook yourself usually have more food value than cold cereals—and are considerably less expensive. If you do buy ready-to-eat cereals, remember that the small boxes containing individual servings can be two or three times as expensive as the same cereal in a larger box.

Whenever possible, use fresh or frozen vegetables instead of starchy products like noodles, macaroni, and spaghetti. The fewer processes a food has gone through, and the fewer things that've been taken out of it, the more nourishment it's likely to still have. When you do want macaroni, noodles, and the like, health food stores have them made from more parts of the grain.

Use brown rice instead of polished white rice—the difference in nourishment is tremendous. When you cook the rice, don't drain it or rinse it; instead use three cups of water for each cup of rice and let the rice absorb the water as it cooks. And use as little water as possible when you cook other things, then try to use the liquid in a soup or stew.

We've also known for a long time that white bread is not the most nutritious of foods—though enriching the flour has helped some and using unbleached flour and no preservatives has helped more. You'll probably want to include some darker breads in your family's diet.

Many women—and men—have taken up baking the family's bread as a hobby. Some have become famous among their friends for their rye bread, others for their whole wheat or pumpernickel. If you bake your own bread, you can use unbleached flour, skip all the preservatives, and turn out a much more nutritious loaf. And you can add all sorts of healthy things like wheat germ, powdered milk, and soy flour. If you have a freezer, it's easy to make a double batch and freeze some.

If you bake your own cookies, you'll know exactly what goes into them—and you can add lots of healthy things like raisins, dates, and nuts.

Have you discovered molasses? It adds a rich, dark taste to many foods—cookies, cakes, breads, baked beans—has almost twice as much iron as beef liver and is more easily digested. It's good on bread and butter, in baked apples, stirred into milk, or mixed with honey as a topping for puddings and desserts. Some people stir one to three tablespoons of molasses into a cup of piping hot water for a healthful and interesting coffee substitute.

And, speaking of coffee, many people are finding that they feel better if they switch from coffee and tea (which contain caffeine) to one of the delightful teas sold by health food stores. Or to milk.

Many people also are trying to use honey in place of sugar. Unlike sugar, honey doesn't leave a residue of impurities, so it doesn't leave a person feeling tired later. It also has vitamins and minerals, is easily digested, and is both a soother and an energizer.

Honey is good on hot cereals, toast, pancakes, waffles, French toast, fresh fruits (especially on a watermelon that needs more sweetness), ice cream (add a few nuts), and is excellent for canning and freezing. It also helps baked goods stay fresh longer—use it to replace half the sugar called for in the recipe.

God is our refuge and strength, a very
present help in trouble.
Psalms

SNACKS

Getting the family to eat healthful snack foods can sometimes be a problem. Some people think only in terms of candy, soft drinks, deep-fat-fried concoctions, and pastries. These are expensive, can lead to bigger dentist's bills, and offer little in the way of nourishment. If they're allowed to take the place of good food in a family's diet, health can suffer.

For healthier snacks try raisins and dried fruits, fresh fruit, and fruit juices. These are expensive too, but when you consider that, unlike the empty-calorie foods they'll be replacing, they offer real nutrition, they are not unreasonable. Also good are peanuts and nuts of all kinds; milk; sunflower seeds and other seeds; carrots, celery, and other vegetables; and breads, rolls, and cookies made with natural ingredients.

So keep raw vegetables and fruits handy and ready to eat in your refrigerator. Researchers have found that people who eat two apples a day have 35% fewer colds. An apple a day can keep the doctor away—and the psychiatrist (apples are a natural tranquilizer).

Packing a lunch or snacks for school or work can be money-saving and can also let you enjoy more healthy foods. Few vending machines offer any very nutritious snacks. Brown-bagging can also help you keep your weight where you want it.

WEIGHT

The California researchers found that keeping a proper weight can help prolong life. Surprisingly they found that those who were 5 to 10% overweight had a lower death rate than those who were underweight. Those more than 20% overweight had the highest death rate.

EXERCISE

The seventh item in the California good health list is moderate exercise. If the fuel shortage makes it necessary for us to walk instead of riding so much, this can be all to the good.

Most of us balk at exercises that take 15 to 30 minutes a day—even though we know we need them. Would you believe that there is a set of exercises that is pleasant and easy and takes only 3 to 4 minutes *a week?* At the end of six months—and a grand total of only 78 to 104 minutes of exercise—some people find they've taken several inches off around their midsection, flattened their abdomen noticeably, and are able to pull in their stomach for the first time in their life. They also have better posture and look and feel better.

Here's how the exercises are done, each for 6-8 seconds:

1. Stand tall, pulling your abdomen in (and continue to pull it in as you do each of the exercises), and, linking your hands together, press the inside of your hands against your forehead and your forehead against your hands.

2. Press the palm of your right hand against the right side of your head and the right side of your head against your right hand.
3. Do the same with your left hand and the left side of your head.
4. This next one looks silly—grit your teeth, pulling up the muscles in your chest with those in your jaw and neck. Keep doing this for the full 6-8 seconds.
5. Placing the heels of your hands together, press one hand against the other as hard as you can.
6. Clasp your hands together, then try to pull them apart without actually pulling them apart.
7. Put your left foot against the left side of a regular-size doorway, your right foot against the right side. Now push your feet against the door frame as hard as you can.
8. Put your feet against the outside of the two front legs of a chair and pull your feet toward each other as hard as you can. (This is the reverse of 7. Some people do exercises 5 and 8 together, then 6 and 7 together, saving a few seconds.)
9. Placing the toes of your right foot a few inches out from the wall and your right hand and forearm on the wall in front of you, press your right hand against the wall.
10. Do the same with your left hand and foot.

It's not necessary to do these exercises every day—every other day is better. If you do them faithfully Monday, Wednesday, Friday, and Sunday of each week for six months (being sure to pull in your abdomen firmly as you do each one), you should have to take in the waistline of all your clothes a few inches.

By the time you've done them for a year or so, a woman can often throw away her girdle and a man can stop thinking that he really should get himself one—all from only a little more than three hours of exercise. (For more exercises, see Clement G. Martin's *How to Stay Young All Your Life.*)

SHOWERS

To continue to live well during an energy shortage we may have to cut down a little on the length of the showers we take—or on the depth of the water, if we prefer the tub. Or we can take more sponge baths. Someone has calculated that the average shower requires 5 gallons of water, while the average bath takes 10. Perhaps bath takers could switch to a shower occasionally—or discover that they can still have a refreshing bath with considerably less water.

Either way, we'll have to cut down on the amount of water we use. At the present time we're using four times our weight in water every day, and industry uses an equal amount for each of us. By the end of this century these figures are expected to double—if that much water can be found.

PERSONAL CARE

Many families have found out that, instead of packing all the kids into the family car for a trip to the barber shop, with an inexpensive hair cutting kit containing shears, clippers, comb, plastic cape for over the shoulders and a brush for whisking away hairs, they can save both gas and wear and tear on the car—and a lot of money as well.

Some husbands and wives have also become good at trimming up each other's hair and neckline.

Some women find getting together and giving each other a permanent a good way to save a trip to the beauty shop—and money. And a good chance to do a little visiting.

Whenever possible, avoid buying hair spray, deodorants, and other products that come in a spray can; some people have had strong allergic reactions to these—and they add a lot of volume to our already overworked garbage disposal areas.

Good health habits do pay off. Living by the basic seven habits can increase your days and add greatly to the pleasure you get out of life.

● ● ●

You are the temple of God.
Paul

Heating
and
Cooling

In Lancaster County, Pennsylvania a religious group called the House Amish have chosen to do without electricity and seem to be living very comfortable, happy lives without all the electric appliances that we sometimes think essential—roasters, shavers, hair dryers, can openers, knife sharpeners, bottle warmers, nail buffers. They cook their delicious apple dishes on a wood stove, sharpen their knives on a whetstone, and whip their cream with a hand beater. And so no rivers are spoiled providing electricity for them.

They have also chosen to live without cars and other gasoline-powered machinery, and sometimes motorists who pass them in their horse and buggy along a back country road are apt to feel superior—while enshrouding them in a cloud of smoke and fumes that leaves man and beast reeling and makes it harder for the nearby crops to grow.

The Amish use windmills to pump water from deep wells into cisterns, then hand pumps to bring the water from the cistern into the house.

They have also chosen to do without radios and TV.

And, since they have no indoor plumbing, they cause no sewage disposal problems.

So almost nothing in their whole way of life causes any real pollution.

If all the world lived as they do, we would have no fuel shortages and no serious pollution problems. Our air would be marvelously fresh, our waterways sparkling and our soil fertile and ready to provide us with foods that would be both satisfying and nourishing.

If we want to survive on this planet, we're going to have to learn all we can from people who know how to live in harmony with the earth—and we're going to have to put what we learn into practice as quickly as possible. Not that we can do everything the Amish do: most of us have no woodlot with firewood to warm our home and provide fuel for cooking, no fields to raise oats to fuel our horse-drawn transportation, no room for large gardens to produce all our food.

But there are many things that we can learn from them about co-operating with nature, living with it rather than abusing it, respecting it and preserving it rather than destroying it.

As we think about it, we know that there are many things that we can do to return our world to a more livable state and keep it that way.

> Out of the south cometh the whirlwind:
> and the cold out of the north.
>
> Job

HEATING

More than half the energy used in a home is used for heating. One of the best ways to keep this heat in and the cold out is to make sure your home is well insulated—often 15-30% of a house's heat is lost due to poor insulation. A good way to check this is to place a thermometer on the inside surface of an outside wall, then near the center of the room. Leave the thermometer in each place for four hours, and if there's more than five degrees difference between the two readings, you should consider upgrading the insulation in that room.

✥

Ceiling insulation does the most good. Even in regions of the country with relatively mild winters, the cost of ceiling insulation can be returned by fuel savings the first year. Since heat rises, ceiling insulation alone can cut heating expenses by as much as one-third. If your attic floor has no floor boards, you can easily install the insulation yourself.

✠

If air from the house is leaking into the attic, moisture can be going with it and causing problems—condensation can damage insulation and other building materials. A small amount of moisture in the attic can be expelled through air vents, which should be left open in the winter; but the more moisture there is, the harder it is for the outdoor air to ventilate it out.

✠

Ideally a house should have insulation in all exterior side walls as well as in the ceiling. While this is customary in newer homes, it is rarely found in older homes. Insulating finished walls in an existing home is more difficult and normally requires an insulation contractor. Insulation is also useful for floors over crawl spaces.

✠

Check to make sure there is a storm window on each window (unless you have double-pane glass) and a storm door on each door. If winter has already come and it's not possible to install these, tape or nail clear plastic over the window area. Besides reducing heat loss, storm windows also lessen the difference between room air and window temperatures, reducing drafts.

✠

You might want to consider replacing large areas of single-pane glass with double-pane to cut down on heat loss.

✠

Open up the shades, drapes, or curtains each morning to let as much sun in as possible. Close them at sundown and during exceptionally cold periods to keep the house's heat in.

✠

Close the fireplace damper. This can keep a lot of heat from going up the chimney. If the fireplace is no longer in use, install an airtight seal in the chimney.

✠

Check around the inside of doors and windows to see if there's any draft. In fact, check all over the house, inside and out, for places where heat might be escaping. Hardware stores have several types of weatherstripping which are not difficult to apply.

✠

Check for heat leaks around ceiling fixtures, air ducts, and plumbing ducts or pipes.

✠

Don't use your oven to heat your kitchen on a cold morning; it's very expensive, wastes gas, and will do you little good. Ovens do not circulate heat efficiently or economically. They're designed for baking and roasting, not space heating. And many municipal codes prohibit such use.

✠

If your home is brick, check for openings and cracks in the masonry and apply caulking.

✠

If your home is wood, some people recommend soaking it with a garden hose just before the hard freeze in the fall so that the wood will swell and seal out the cold.

✠

An entryway can keep the wintry winds from blowing full blast into your house every time the door is opened.

✠

Be sure furniture isn't blocking registers or cold-air returns. And make sure that all vents, registers, and radiators are clean and free from obstructions. If you have baseboard heating, vacuum the units periodically.

✠

Don't heat rooms you don't need. Shut the doors and shut off the heating to them.

✠

If your basement is heated, be sure the upper wall construction is not open from the basement to the attic, drawing heat out of the basement.

✠

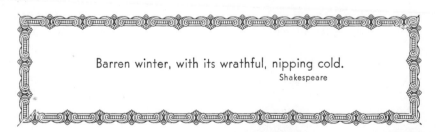

Barren winter, with its wrathful, nipping cold.
Shakespeare

Does your basement really need to be heated? Certainly the heating ducts can be shut off much of the time—and this will make it a better storage area for apples, potatoes, squash, carrots, and other fruits and vegetables, which are less expensive purchased in quantity and stored.

✠

Check the ductwork under the house and in the attic for loose or bent connections. If ductwork is exposed to outside air in an attic or crawl space, seal the joints with insulation tape and wrap the ductwork with insulation so the heat in the air won't be lost on its way to your living area.

✠

If your garage is part of your house, insulate the parts touching the house—and remember to keep the doors shut.

✠

Seal all cracks around attic doors and pulldown stairs.

✠

Close all doors leading from living areas to an unheated basement, attic, or crawl space.

✠

Remind children to close doors immediately when they're entering or leaving the house.

✠

Turning the heat down a few degrees can make everyone feel better if they dress warmly enough. A heavy, long-sleeved sweater—or even two sweaters—can make a person comfortable in even a very cool room. Now's the time to dig out that ski sweater from Norway. If you have an over-the-hip sweater, so much the warmer. A heavy sweater or two in a cooler house may become the new status symbol in energy-short America.

✠

Long warm pants are practical for everyone. Most offices now permit pant suits, and many pant suits are so attractive that they can be worn anywhere—shopping, to church, to parties and receptions. Why should men be the only ones to be comfortable in cold weather?

✠

Cozy long underwear now comes in bright colors for women. A set of this covered by some warm wool pants and a heavy sweater or two should keep even the chilliest girl warm—even if room temperatures get down to 60° or less.

✠

There's a lot of difference in the warmth of shoes—and some come with a fleecy lining and high tops. If your feet tend to be chilly, look into these.

✠

When women must wear dresses for special occasions, there are warm little undershirts that fit very snugly and longer-legged underpants.

✠

Turtleneck sweaters with tops that keep you warm right up to the chin can be the first line of defense for the chilly person.

✠

Stores are showing "Dr. Dentons" for adults again—the long, warm, footed pajamas—just the thing to wear in a cold bedroom.

✠

If you get yourself a good warm coat, hat, scarf, gloves, and boots you won't mind going outside and walking instead of taking the car. And you won't come in chilled to the bone and be tempted to turn up the thermostat.

✠

Setting a thermostat higher than you need to usually will not make an area heat up any faster. If you set it for 72°, your heating system will heat your house to 72° as soon as it can. Setting it at 80° won't help it get there any faster. It will just overheat the house and maybe even make it necessary to open a window and waste heat. If you have a two-step moving air system however, a higher setting will help heat the area faster.

✠

Clean the thermostat once a year by removing the cover and gently blowing the dust out of the mechanism.

✠

If you turn the thermostat down a few degrees this week, let everyone get adjusted, then turn it down a few more degrees a few weeks from now, people can adjust to the new lower temperatures.

✠

Lowering the thermostat setting by 1° can result in a 3-4% reduction in fuel consumption, by 5° in a 15-20% reduction. But don't keep fiddling with the thermostat—constantly adjusting it up and down can waste fuel.

✠

Set your house temperature lower at night. A night set-back clock can do this automatically for you. Doctors say that lowering room temperatures to even as low as 60° will not increase the likelihood of a person's catching a cold, influenza, or pneumonia if he dresses appropriately. Rather the lower temperatures will inhibit the growth of most bacteria, giving a person a better chance of staying healthy.

✠

If you sleep with a window open at night, keep the bedroom door closed and the heat turned down.

✠

An extra blanket and warmer pajamas may make it possible for you to set the thermostat back even farther at night.

✠

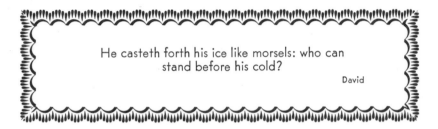

He casteth forth his ice like morsels: who can stand before his cold?

David

A warm robe and slippers can keep you more comfortable for relaxing in a chilly house.

✠

If you have an electric blanket, you may find that turning it on when you start to get ready for bed can warm up the bed enough that you can turn it off for the night. Putting another blanket over your electric blanket will help hold in the heat. Remember to turn off your electric blanket in the morning.

✠

Before the days of central heating, people used to sleep in bedrooms that got so cold that a glass of water on the bedtable would have ice on it in the morning. Were they less healthy? No, they were less like hothouse flowers than we are today. Plants grown in a warm greenhouse aren't very adaptable to any other conditions—they're fragile and perishable, vulnerable to many things. But plants that have been raised in a cool window or outside are ready for whatever comes along. Perhaps it's just as well if our days as hothouse plants are over.

✠

Have your furnace or boiler checked once a year by a qualified furnaceman. Routine maintenance can save on operating costs, prevent breakdowns, and conserve fuel.

✠

Change the filters in your furnace frequently during the heating season. A clogged filter interferes with the flow of air through the furnace, making it less efficient and more expensive to operate. Permanent filters should be vacuumed or washed regularly.

✣

Blowers and blower motors on the furnace require lubrication for peak performance. If there's an oil cup or tube mounted on each side of the blower or motor, give them the lubrication they need, following the manufacturer's recommendations. As a general rule, putting several drops of oil in each cup or tube at the start of the heating season and again halfway through the season should be sufficient. If your lubrication system was sealed at the factory, you need do nothing.

✠

Check the furnace's fan belt to be sure it's not cracked or frayed. If it shows excessive wear, replace it.

✠

If you have a forced-air system and your duct dampers are set for summer cooling, readjust them to the winter setting.

✠

Check your humidifier at the beginning of the heating season to be sure it's clean and operating properly. Check it again several times during the winter, cleaning it whenever necessary.

✣

If you maintain a high level of humidity in your home, you can lower the heat and still feel just as warm. The same humidity that makes you feel warmer in the summer will also make you feel warmer in the winter.

✣

Maintaining the proper humidity can also prevent the discomforts of dry skin and can alleviate sinus, nose, throat, bronchial, and lung conditions.

✣

Hot water heating systems can't function efficiently unless the radiators are full of water; make certain they're full before starting the boiler. If the radiators have air vents, check to make sure all air is eliminated.

• • •

He giveth snow like wool.
David

Is your chimney clean? It's a simple procedure to look up the inside of it at the cleanout opening with a mirror. Be sure it's free of obstructions.

✠

Also check the outside of the chimney for cracks and other signs of deterioration and have them repaired. Proper venting of fumes will keep your family healthier and your furnace more efficient.

✠

Check the flue pipe and draft hood for rust, cracks, or accumulation of soot, making sure that the flue pipe fits securely at all connections and is properly supported.

✠

If the pilot light on your furnace or boiler has been turned off for the summer, be sure to follow the relighting procedures shown on the heating equipment. If you have any problems in starting up your furnace or boiler in the fall or saw any signs of trouble during your inspection, it's best to call in an experienced repairman.

✠

Keep the operating manual for your furnace or boiler on a nearby nail for handy reference. In addition to explaining the warranty, it will give you instructions that will make the equipment easier to maintain.

✠

If you find it necessary to use a portable electric heater, be sure it's thermostatically controlled and limit its use to temporary spot heating. These units use a lot of energy and are not designed for full-time heating.

✠

Rooms often become too hot when there are many people in them, so when you're going to be entertaining, reduce the setting a few degrees before the guests arrive.

✠

If your house is cold, have a party.

✠

When you're building a new house, consider how to get the most heating from the sun during the winter. Facing the house toward the west and south accomplishes this best. Wooden slat roof overhangs above the windows can let in the low winter sun and keep out the high summer sun.

✠

Get the right size furnace for your needs. A unit that is larger than necessary costs more to begin with and wastes fuel. Too small a unit will be strained and is apt to wear out sooner.

Make sure your thermostat is away from sources of cold or heat such as windows, heating ducts, TVs, lamps, doors that open to the outside.

Thou hast made summer and winter.
Psalms

COOLING

If you don't have an air conditioner, perhaps you can avoid getting one by adding insulation to the house; by installing awnings, canopies or roof overhangs; by closing the blinds and curtains during the hot part of the day; by using well-placed fans around the house and in the attic to draw out the hot air.

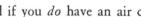

Planting shade trees can be very helpful. One good shade tree can do the work of ten room air conditioners. Trees that lose their leaves are best so they can let the warm sunlight into the house in the winter. And select trees whose branches curve upward rather than downward; a tree with drooping branches can trap the heat.

If windows can't be protected from the outside from direct sunlight, use light-colored opaque draperies. By keeping these closed when the window is exposed to direct sunlight you can reduce the sun's heating of your home by 50%.

All these suggestions are also good if you *do* have an air conditioner.

If you can't shade a window from the outside and don't want to cover it with draperies, consider installing heat-absorbing or reflecting glass. This can reduce heat entering the house by 70%. But it also blocks out the sunlight during the winter when you might like the additional warmth.

Leave the storm windows on windows that are not going to be opened during the summer months—this helps keep the heat out. But even with the storm windows on you'll need to shade the windows in some way.

✠

In the summer try to schedule heat-generating activities such as cooking, vacuuming, washing, and ironing for the cooler evening hours.

✠

If you don't have them, construct exterior vents for major appliances such as stoves and clothes dryers. The more hot air you send outside, the cooler your house will be. Check the filters for these regularly and replace them when necessary.

✠

After bathing turn on the bathroom exhaust fan or open the bathroom window, making sure the bathroom door is closed, to get rid of the warm, moist air.

✠

Cut down on the amount of hot water you use for laundry, showering, and bathing, and the house will stay cooler.

✠

Turn off any lights that are not needed—they add heat and use up energy.

✠

Also save moisture-producing activities for cooler times of the day. Mopping, dishwashing, washing clothes, and baking all increase the humidity and make a person feel warmer.

✠

An attic fan is helpful even if you have air conditioning. When the temperature is 95° outside, the temperature in your attic can be as high as 130°. This layer of heat makes it more difficult to cool your living space. An attic fan that pulls the hot, dead air out through a window or through a vent in a gable, wall, or roof can reduce the attic temperature as much as 35°. Your air conditioner doesn't have to work as hard when it's not battling a hot attic.

✠

If you do use an air conditioner, set the controls so that the air is cooled but not chilled. Instead of having the house icy cold and putting on sweaters, dress as lightly as people do who have no air conditioning, then set the thermostat accordingly.

✠

Each degree you raise your thermostat can save you about 5% of the cost of operating your air conditioning.

✠

Many days you may not need to run the air conditioner at all. Turn it off as much as you can.

✠

At night raise your air conditioner's setting by several degrees.

✠

Some families have both a central air conditioning system and a window unit in the bedroom. At night they turn off the central system and turn on the window unit to cool the bedroom.

✠

Few things are more ridiculous than a family that turns the furnace on in the morning to take the slight chill out of the air, then turns the air conditioner on in the afternoon and puts on sweaters. On a beautiful day you may have heard a neighbor say, "It's so nice today that I can't decide whether to turn on the furnace or the air conditioner."

✠

Cooler clothing can greatly increase your comfort in warm weather. When will offices start allowing the men to work without coats so that the air conditioning can be turned to a warmer setting and the women can stop being chilly even with heavy sweaters on?

✠

> Come, summer, come, the sweet season and sun!
> James I of Scotland

Many times even though the outside air is a trifle warmer than the ideal, having it blowing gently through the house will be more refreshing than shutting up the house completely and turning the air conditioning on.

✠

Most of the suggestions in the section on heating that refer to keeping heat *in* the house in winter also apply to keeping heat *out* of the house in the summer: having proper insulation, keeping the fireplace damper closed, checking for cracks and other air leaks and stopping them, keeping ductwork clean, keeping obstructions away from registers, having ductwork insulated, using double- instead of single-pane glass in windows, keeping the air conditioner in good repair.

✠

Don't get a larger air conditioner than you need. Too large a unit will cool the house before it has removed all the moisture from the air. A unit just slightly smaller than space requirements call for will give the best service.

✠

Keep your air conditioner in good working order. Before using it, check and lubricate the bearings as recommended in the manufacturer's manual. Check the filters every 30 days when it's being used, and replace them when necessary. Also check for proper tension and wear on all pulley belts.

✠

If you have central air conditioning with an outdoor condenser, keep it free of leaves, grass, and anything else that may block the air flow.

✠

If you're going to repaint or reshingle your house, use a light color. The sun can make dark surfaces as much as 60° warmer than the surrounding air, while a light surface will only be made 20° warmer.

✠

If you use window air conditioners, use fans to reduce the need for more units. Fans can distribute cool air from rooms with window units to rooms without them, increasing the area of effectiveness for an air conditioner without a great increase in power consumption.

✠

Be sure your window air conditioners are protected from the direct sun or their efficiency will be reduced. Either place them on the north or shady side of the house or shade them from the sun.

✠

If you have window air conditioning units and a central heating furnace, cover or close the floor or side wall registers and low-return grills while the air conditioning is on. Cool air settles and can escape through these openings.

✠

If you have only one window air conditioning unit in the house, keep the room cool by opening and closing the door as seldom as possible.

Keep the grills on your window air conditioning units clean, being careful not to damage the evaporator coils or fins. If your unit has an air filter close to the cooling coil, keep it clean to prevent a buildup of dirt and frost that would hinder the proper flow of air.

If a room with a window air conditioning unit will be unoccupied for several hours, set the control at a higher temperature or turn the unit off entirely.

If Winter comes, can Spring be far behind?
Shelley

WATER HEATERS

Heating water accounts for about 15% of your home's total utility bill, so cut down its use wherever you can.

The size of your water heater should match your needs. An oversized water heater wastes energy heating unneeded water.

In building a new home or remodeling an older one, locate your water heater close to the points of use. Shorter pipe runs mean less heat loss and lower costs.

Be sure the pipes from your water heater are insulated to prevent loss of heat.

Perhaps your water heater could be turned down a few degrees, saving energy and money.

Quickly repair any leaky faucets around the house—they can let gallons of hot water drip away every day.

When you turn a faucet off, be sure to turn it all the way off.

✠

When washing dishes, do not leave the hot water faucet running continuously for rinsing. Rather run a small amount in a pan and dip the dishes in or put the clean dishes in a drain basket and rinse them all at once under the faucet.

✠

When you're shaving, don't let the hot water run constantly—turn it on only when it's needed.

✠

It's a good idea to flush out your hot water heater tank at least once a year to get rid of rust and lime deposits. This can prolong the life of the unit and give it a higher operating efficiency.

✠

Turn off your hot water heater when you're going to be away from home for a length of time.

✠

The day may be coming when we'll have the water heater on only one or two days a week.

LIGHTING

Turn off all unused lights.

✠

Reduce light intensities wherever you can. One family put smaller bulbs in many of their outlets and eliminated 600 unneeded watts. This also made their lighting in areas where it didn't have to be bright more subtle and dramatic.

✠

Use Christmas and other holiday decorations that don't require lights.

✠

Turn off all gas and electric outdoor lights that are used purely for aesthetic purposes.

✠

Substitute fluorescent for incandescent lights wherever you can. They use only about half the electricity and their life span can be ten times as long.

✠

If you must have outdoor lighting, use a photoelectric cell to turn the lights on and off automatically so they're not on when they're not needed. Timers can perform the same task but must be reset repeatedly to allow for changes in the time of sunrise and sunset.

Be sure to turn out the lights when you leave a room (unless there's someone else in it).

There is no surge of power when a light is turned on. If a bulb is on for two seconds, it uses only two seconds' worth of electricity.

Now and then inspect for overloaded outlets, faulty light switches, and frayed cords. It's better to repair these before a fire occurs.

VACATIONS

Use a timer (or ask a neighbor) to turn a few lights on and off in the evening to discourage break-ins rather than leaving the lights on all the time you're gone.

Make sure all the gas outlets in your home are closed before you leave. Keeping pilot lights going can account for one-tenth of the gas bill in a normal month. If there are any you want working when you return, have a neighbor turn them on before you reach home.

If you vacation in the winter, set the thermostat at the lowest setting. Where there is no danger of water pipes freezing, heating systems can be turned off completely.

If you vacation in the summer, turn off your air conditioner. Also turn off your water heater.

While driving, remember to slow down to save gas.

Try to use your automobile air conditioner as little as possible. Have it cleaned and checked before you leave.

If you can avoid driving during the hottest parts of the day, you can avoid using the air conditioner so much.

Set your air conditioner at the warmest level that is still comfortable.

In the summer choose sites for your trailer or camper that have natural shade. And open your windows at night.

Check the propane or butane lines in your trailer or camper for leaks and turn off all outlets before traveling.

If you have a trailer or camper, slow down; your speed affects your gas mileage even more than if you were in a car. Relax and have a more pleasant vacation.

While the earth remaineth, seedtime and harvest, and cold and heat, and summer and winter, and day and night shall not cease.

Genesis

The Kitchen

Great-grandma turned out a remarkable array of foods in her kitchen: spicy watermelon pickles, fragrant banana bread, creamy vanilla pudding, baked hams studded with cloves. She would be astonished if she could step into one of our kitchens today and see all the frivolous electric gadgets crowded together on the counters and crammed into the cupboards.

"What's the matter?" she might ask. "Can't people lift a finger to do anything for themselves any more?"

After this remark we might avoid taking her past the river polluted by the waste from the power plant, or out into the country where strip mining to secure coal for the power plant makes the area look wartorn. She might ask if it was all worth it, and I'm afraid we couldn't give her a positive answer.

APPLIANCES

If you're thinking of buying more electric gadgets for your kitchen, ask yourself, "Can't I get along just as well without an electric knife sharpener, can opener, carving knife, orange squeezer, or whatever it is? Will this really save me that much time? Couldn't I use the exercise anyway? And wouldn't I rather preserve the environment so my grandchildren will have a chance for a livable world?"

Researchers have found that if every home in the nation that now has an electric can opener didn't get it repaired the next time it breaks down, enough energy would be saved to meet the complete electrical needs of 40,000 homes. The same probably goes for the many other electrical devices that we could so easily do without.

✠

Before you buy any appliance for your kitchen, compare its usefulness with the energy it would consume.

✠

When you're purchasing a new stove or refrigerator, see how many of the optional extras you can do without. A frost-free refrigerator, for instance, uses 50% more energy than a standard model.

✠

Make sure the pilot light on your gas stove is adjusted properly. It could be using more fuel than it needs to.

✠

Be sure your gas stove isn't leaking, wasting fuel and endangering your family's health. If there's a gas smell (except briefly when you light a burner), call a repairman.

✠

Pilot lights on stoves and ovens can be turned off completely. After they are, you need only light a match to light a burner. This can save you 10% on your gas bill for these appliances.

✠

If you don't have a garbage disposal in your sink, don't buy one. With even a very small space outside for growing things you can dig in your potato peelings, apple cores, orange rinds, the outer leaves of lettuce, and such. These can even be worked into the soil in a planter to enrich it.

✠

Turn on the cold water before you turn on your garbage disposal. And after you've turned off the motor, let the water run a while to clean out the trap in the pipe.

✠

Don't use chemical drain cleaners if you have a garbage disposal. They can damage metal and rubber parts.

✠

When you do buy a new appliance, read the manual that comes with it carefully so you'll know how to care for it properly.

✠

Set aside a kitchen drawer or shelf for keeping the manuals for your appliances so you can refer to them when necessary.

When you use an appliance, occasionally check the plug and cord as you plug it in to be sure it's in good repair.

At housecleaning time check all appliances, cleaning, oiling, and making repairs where necessary.

When an appliance does wear out, see if you could get along without replacing it.

> Beware of little Expenses:
> a small Leak will sink a great Ship.
> Benjamin Franklin

CUPBOARDS

Keeping your spice boxes in alphabetical order from Anise to Zesty Red Pepper can help you find them quickly and easily. You're more apt to use them, food will taste better, and your family will enjoy meals more.

Other things can also be alphabetized on shelves—canned goods, cereals, dessert items.

Keep potatoes and onions in a cool, dark place, not under the sink. It's too warm and moist.

Don't keep too many kinds of cereal on hand at once. Have a few and use them up, then buy more. This can prevent all those half-empty boxes of cereal too old to eat.

Fold down the inner wrapping in the cereal package before closing the box to keep the cereal fresh and crisp.

✠

Don't have your cupboards so full that you can't see what's in them and things go to waste.

✠

If you have the problem of bread molding before you get the whole loaf used up, put half of it into a heavy plastic bag and into the freezer. This way you should almost never have to throw out old bread.

✠

Save and re-use plastic bags such as bread wrappers for storing things. You can also cut them open to use for covering things instead of buying plastic wrap.

✠

Aluminum foil can often be rinsed off and re-used.

✠

Instead of buying lunch sacks, use those you get shopping. Many ecology-minded brown-baggers fold up their lunch sacks and bring them home each day to use again.

✠

Store things like oatmeal, flour, and sugar that are tempting to small creatures in jars or canisters.

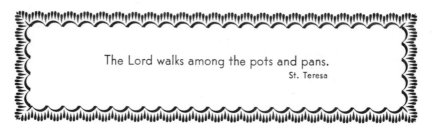

The Lord walks among the pots and pans.
St. Teresa

EATING

Avoid using paper and plastic throwaway products whenever possible. These plates, glasses, silver, napkins, and other disposable items are overwhelming our nation's waste disposal system—and they require a lot of energy to produce.

✠

We'll also save several cents a meal for each person by not using these throwaway items. But what will we do with the money we save? If we turn around and spend it on something else that requires energy to make and will create a problem to dispose of, we really haven't gained. Can we direct our spending toward items that are not as hard on the environment?

If your family is still drinking soft drinks—these are not the most nourishing items, they demand a lot in the way of packaging, and they create an enormous disposal problem—make sure they don't leave the pull rings where fish and birds will swallow them and die.

Napkin rings with the owner's name can come in handy as we go back to using cloth napkins. Your children might enjoy making one for each member of the family from wood, straw, cardboard, or whatever is handy.

When the plastic seats and backs on your kitchen chairs begin to crack, rip, or develop holes, instead of throwing them out, repair them.

If the rips are minor, get some of the attractive cut-outs made to prevent slipping in the bathtub (they'll keep people from slipping off the chair as well). These will stop rips from becoming bigger and come in several sizes so that you can cover all sorts of holes. And they add a decorative touch. Choose colors to match or contrast with your chairs.

If the seats and backs of the chairs are too worn to be repaired, buy new plastic and recover them. This is not difficult. Turn the chair upside down—most seats unscrew from the bottom. Stretch the plastic over the seat, fasten it on with tacks or staples, then screw the seat back on. Do the same with the back.

Do we really need a tablecloth that needs to be washed and ironed on the table every day? Most tables are so attractive that they need no covering up. As our country emerged from its pioneer days, the tablecloth became a symbol that a family was able to live above the mere subsistence level, that it was able to enjoy the finer things of life. Now, in an effort to keep the world livable for our children and grandchildren, the tablecloth may become a symbol once more—by its absence.

DISHWASHING

To have a dishwasher or not to have a dishwasher—that is the question. Whether 'tis nobler to save hot water by using the dishwasher instead of washing dishes by hand—or to save electricity by washing dishes by hand instead of using the dishwasher. Perhaps the times are out of joint.

✠

Much less hot water is required to wash dishes all at once automatically than to wash them a few at a time by hand after each meal.

✠

Don't run your dishwasher until you have a full load. Rinse the dishes off and set them in after each meal; modern dishwashers will get them clean. This saves fuel and hot water.

✠

If you need more dishes in order to have the dishwasher full before you run it, try your local thrift shop. This helps recycle things and gives jobs to the handicapped. A neighbor who took weeks to work up the courage to go in now visits it every now and then and is as proud of the additions she has made to her set as if she were out looking for some rare antique pieces to complete a collection.

✠

Some dishwashers have a partial load cycle that allows you to do less than a full load with proportionately less water.

✠

Load your dishwasher correctly to insure thorough washing of each item and prevent having to wash some items again.

✠

Use enough detergent to insure proper cleaning, but not so much that dishes are left with a soapy smell.

✠

Debris in the dishwasher pump can hamper the machine's efficiency. Scraping food from plates—especially bones and seeds—can prevent this problem.

✠

Check the filter screen over the drain in the dishwasher regularly and remove any particles.

✠

Although plates can be warmed in the dishwasher, it's more saving of fuel to put them in the oven and use the heat left from cooking the meal.

You can save electricity by washing dishes by hand. This is more work —perhaps as much as 25 8-hour days a year extra for the average family—but it saves a factory from having to turn out a dishwasher, saves you from having to buy one, and is wonderful for warming up the hands in the winter.

A merry heart doeth good like a medicine.
Proverbs

THE SINK

The plastic mesh bags that some vegetables come in can be folded up and held together with a few stitches to make excellent pot scrubbers.

Use the smallest amount of water you can for each job. And never let the water run endlessly.

If the hot water takes too long in coming, your pipes may need insulating between the water heater and the sink.

Don't put oil, grease, or chemicals down the drain—this includes prescription medications and other medicines that you're throwing out. Put them in the garbage instead so they won't add an additional burden on our already burdened waterways.

For the same reason it's better not to use the garbage disposal if you can possibly avoid using it. If you can't dig your peels and rinds into your garden, put them in the garbage can. Our lakes and rivers already have enough to contend with.

You can save a lot of water by bending the arm down on your toilet tank float. It will use less water, yet operate with the same efficiency.

CLEANING EQUIPMENT

You can avoid a lot of scrubbing and keep your rugs and carpet cleaner by placing mats outside all doors (and just inside them, too).

✠

Sponge mops will last many times as long if you rinse them under running water until the water runs clear after using them. Chemicals left in the sponge can cause rapid deterioration.

✠

Keep products on hand to take out stains immediately—before they have a chance to set. Some stains require only common household items—cold water for blood, ice for chewing gum, warm water for coffee or chocolate. But for all-around use you'll need four types of removers:

1. An absorbent powder like cornstarch to soak up grease spots
2. A detergent to remove many non-greasy and some greasy spots
3. A solvent to dissolve many greasy and some non-greasy spots
4. A bleach

✠

Using stain removers can save you many trips to the cleaners.

✠

If you have pets, keep white vinegar in your cleaning closet to prevent accidents on carpets or upholstered furniture from causing a permanent stain. As soon as possible clean the area with water and rug shampoo, pour on some vinegar and work it into the nap. You might want to test a corner of the rug or furniture first for color fastness, but most good carpets and upholstery will not be harmed.

Some cleaning and maintenance items that you use only rarely can be rented more economically than owning and storing them—rug shampooers, high ladders, sanders, and other power tools.

Empty the bag on your vacuum cleaner frequently to keep the machine working at peak efficiency. Paper vacuum cleaner bags can be cut open, emptied, paper-clipped shut, and used again and again.

✠

When you empty the bag, clean out the filter to keep dirt out of the motor.

Check the vacuum cleaner's brush occasionally and remove threads and hair that have become wound around it. The vacuum cleaner will do a much better job of picking up.

Many of today's linoleums do not need to be waxed, so save yourself time and money—and save on the energy needed to manufacture, transport, and retail the wax—by merely washing and rinsing your floor. A non-slippery floor is safer, too.

You'll probably want to take down cobwebs around your house, but remember that spiders are friends. The house that has spiders usually doesn't have any other small uninvited things. The webs may be a little unsightly—beautiful, actually, but not in the best traditions of good housekeeping—so you'll probably want to remove them if they're someplace where they show. But don't kill the spiders.

Many people use moistened newspapers for cleaning windows. They say the newsprint gives windows a special sparkle.

Keep all cleaning materials out of the reach of children to prevent their accidentally eating or drinking them.

Be careful when working with household chemicals to have proper ventilation. Do these jobs outside in the fresh air or open all the windows whenever possible. Don't pollute your own house with sprays, paints, stains, or cleaning fluids. Some people have found themselves taking months to get well after refinishing the kitchen cupboards in the middle of winter.

Be sure to read the labels and follow directions carefully when using household chemicals. It would be foolish to end up with the house improved and the people in it harmed.

Be careful about smoking around household chemicals—some are quite explosive. And are you sure you want to go on polluting the air in your house, jeopardizing the health of your family?

The kitchen is a good place to start conserving energy.

The Refrigerator

How grandma would have loved to have had one of our modern refrigerators in her kitchen to keep all kinds of foods cool and fresh without carting them out to the wellhouse. A refrigerator is certainly one of the most helpful things we have in our homes; using it wisely can help it serve us well and consume as little fuel as possible.

✠

Before planning and cooking a meal, look in the refrigerator to see what's on hand that needs to be used. But don't hold the door open too long. Take a good look, then shut it while you decide.

✠

If you have the problem of not being able to tell what's in all the containers in your refrigerator, you might want to invest in some clear plastic boxes that are pie-shaped and revolve on a round tray. There's no need to open their lids to see what's inside, and by spinning the tray you can see each of them. With two sets of these you can keep ten different foods in view.

✠

Use fresh foods as soon as possible. Nutritive value can be greatly reduced if foods are stored too long.

✠

Keep staples like pickles, jams, and salad dressings on the back of the shelves, leaving the front for foods that must be used up sooner.

✠

Don't open the refrigerator more often than you really need to. After a meal gather all the things you're going to be putting back on the counter next to it, then open the door and put everything in at once.

✠

Give your refrigerator a break by not putting in foods that don't need to be there. Unless foods like jelly, pickles, peanut butter, and mustard say on the label that they must be refrigerated after opening, they can be kept in the cupboard.

✠

If it's used wisely, a refrigerator doesn't need to be large; what we consider a small refrigerator is the standard size in Europe. By using up leftovers promptly and not refrigerating things that don't need it, you can probably get along with a considerably smaller refrigerator than most people think necessary.

✠

Cool all foods except chicken and other fowl before putting them in the refrigerator to save it work. Poultry spoils easily and needs to be refrigerated quickly.

✠

Do not leave foods such as milk in the warm air too long or they'll lose their freshness faster and also make the refrigerator work harder cooling them again.

✠

Cover everything that you put into the refrigerator to keep flavors from mingling, bacteria from getting in, and foods from drying out and burdening the refrigerator with additional moisture.

✠

Put fresh vegetables that need to be kept moist in the hydrator. If this is full, seal them in plastic bags.

✠

Don't let moisture accumulate in the bottom of the hydrator. Vegetables should be moist but not wet.

✠

Food will taste better and keep longer if you take it out of the can and put it in a plastic box before putting it into the refrigerator.

✠

Hunger is the best pickle.
Benjamin Franklin

Never put anything in the refrigerator that you know you won't use again.

✠

If we make more ice than we really need, a large part of it will evaporate, giving the refrigerator more work.

✠

Filling the refrigerator too full can block the circulation of air and reduce efficiency. Leave space around each item.

✠

Keep a grocery list in the kitchen for jotting down things as you run out of them. Then when you go to the store, you'll know what you need and can avoid buying all sorts of things that you don't need.

✠

The easiest way to keep a refrigerator in order is to straighten it up once a week, using up leftovers and throwing out what can't be used. This way foods won't have a chance to get old.

✠

Leftover meats and vegetables can often be used in an end-of-the-week soup or stew. You can start with a commercially canned one, adding whatever you have on hand.

✠

When you straighten out your refrigerator each week, notice what foods you seem to be throwing out regularly and try to change your buying habits. Perhaps you need to buy smaller packages or cans of things—or make a greater effort to use things up.

✠

When the ice in the refrigerator or freezer gets about ¼-inch thick, it's time to defrost.

✠

If you have a non-frost or self-defrosting refrigerator, examine the drain to make sure it's clean. If it's blocked, ice can build up on the coils and impair the unit's operation.

✠

When you put things into the freezer compartment of your refrigerator, make sure to leave enough space around the control box for the air to circulate or the freezer won't be able to operate properly.

✠

Be sure the door on your refrigerator and freezer is closing tightly to keep the cold air in. To check this, place a dollar bill between the rubber gasket that seals the door and the cabinet and close the door with normal force. When you pull the dollar bill straight out, there should be at least a slight drag. Test all around the door and if there are places where you can feel no drag, call the repairman.

✠

Your refrigerator and freezer door should shut by itself to cut down the time it's open. If it doesn't shut fast enough, adjust the leveling screws under the corners until it does.

✠

The coils on the back of the refrigerator should be kept clean for efficient operation. Unplug the refrigerator, roll it out from the wall and vacuum or dust off the coils whenever they need it. On newer refrigerators these coils are on the bottom; remove the front grill to vacuum them.

✠

Putting your refrigerator on dolly wheels will make it easier to move and clean.

✠

Check to be sure that nothing has fallen behind the refrigerator, obstructing the air circulation through the coils.

✠

Keep the refrigerator as far from the wall as the manual calls for to give it space to operate properly.

✠

Don't have your refrigerator set to run colder than necessary.

✠

A refrigerator will use less energy if it's located away from stoves, ovens, heating equipment, and direct sunlight.

✠

Keep a bottle of touch-up enamel on hand in the color of your refrigerator to take care of nicks and scratches. It comes in a small bottle with a brush and is as easy to use as nail polish. This keeps your refrigerator looking attractive and prevents rust.

When you go on vacation, leave your refrigerator fairly empty and put it on a warmer setting. If you're going to be gone long, turn it off, clean it out, and leave it open.

Follow the manufacturer's directions to give the longest possible life to your refrigerator. If you give it the care it needs, it can serve you better and longer.

Man shall not live by bread alone.
Jesus

Shopping

Great-grandma would have been appalled to have heard the contestant on the TV game show, asked what her hobby was, answer, "Shopping."

Maybe the contestant had a large family and a lot of shopping to do and had decided to make a game of it, trying to get the most value she could for each dollar she spent. But most likely not. She probably saw nothing greater in life than getting and spending.

Shopping seems to have become a pastime for many people, but this is nothing new. Several hundred years ago in *Pilgrim's Progress* John Bunyan cautioned against the folly of being too attracted to Vanity Fair.

Only today it has graver consequences. When we spend money for a lot of frivolous, unnecessary things, we're depleting the world of scarce raw materials. And in disposing of these possessions when we tire of them, we create a further strain on a world that's already overloaded with garbage.

And besides, possessions can become a burden.

Consider the woman who spent her life buying and buying until every cupboard and closet and drawer and storeroom in her house was filled to overflowing. As she lay dying she said to a friend, "What did it all amount to anyway? It was all just junk."

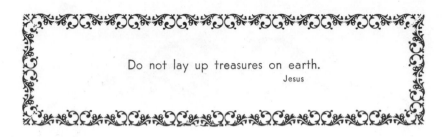

Do not lay up treasures on earth.
Jesus

For the person who moves frequently, too many possessions can be a real problem.

And for the person who becomes seriously ill.

Possessions invite burglaries, they can require a lot of work cleaning and caring for them and they can keep a person from having time for people.

Do we really enjoy wasting away our lives looking endlessly at things? People are more important than things. There are people around us who need us—our families, our friends, our neighbors, people we don't know yet. If one-tenth of the energy that goes into unnecessary shopping every day were put into volunteer work in hospitals and schools, two groups would be happier: those who did the work and those who received the help.

✠

Some shopping is necessary. The person who does it wisely will benefit himself and those who will live in the world he leaves them.

✠

Try to consolidate your shopping trips so that you aren't driving to the store repeatedly for separate items. Keep a running grocery list in the kitchen.

✠

Keep a shopping list in your billfold on which you jot down needed household items. Then when you're near a store, you can stop in without making a special trip.

✠

A grocery cart is a good investment. With it you can save driving to the grocery and laundry and other stores and get some of the fresh air and exercise you need.

✠

Many people are carrying string bags to put their purchases in. This can save a lot of brown paper bags over a few years.

✠

118

Some people fold up their grocery sacks when they get home and take them with them the next time they go shopping, using them again and again.

✠

Now that stores that used to double-bag groceries are putting them in single bags (this had to come), taking your own double bags with you to the store can keep sacks from ripping if you have to carry them very far.

✠

Think before you buy. Maybe after you've thought about it for a while, you won't really want the thing after all.

✠

Sometimes when a child wants something and is allowed to buy it right away, he soon wishes he had bought something else. To prevent this, some families require that a child wait a specified time before buying something with his money. If he still wants the item the next day (or week or month or whatever time is set), he's allowed to buy it. Children are often much happier with this arrangement—and adults might be, too.

✠

If you have a freezer, you can take advantage of special prices on food.

✠

Never buy anything on sale that you don't really want or like or need. Even if something is a good buy, it's not necessarily a good buy for you.

✠

Watch for sales at the end of the season to buy expensive items like appliances, furniture, and clothing. The savings can be tremendous.

✠

Garage sales, estate sales and auctions help recycle things and are great for both buyer and seller—and fun.

✠

Take advantage of fruits and vegetables as they come into season. Prices will be more reasonable.

✠

If you buy soft drinks, ask your grocer to stock re-usable bottles and avoid the disposal problem.

✠

A grocery store's own brand is often a little less expensive than name brands—and just as good.

✠

Avoid buying paper products whenever possible. Spare that tree. We could probably get along with a lot fewer paper towels, plates, napkins, cups, and similar items.

✠

But it's better to buy things in paper than in plastic. A cardboard carton will quickly disintegrate into the soil; a plastic one will lie there endlessly. Ask your grocer to sell things in paper rather than plastic whenever he can—eggs, for instance.

✠

Until he switches over, you can always use the plastic egg cartons to keep small things organized in the kitchen, bedroom, bathroom, den, or workroom. The small compartments are excellent for ear rings, buttons, screws, paper clips, faucet washers, and safety pins.

✠

Perhaps we need more legislation to protect the consumer. Why are rain hats allowed to be sold that shrink the first time you wear them out in the rain? Vacuum cleaners that fall apart before they're two years old (just after their one-year warranty runs out)? Why are buttons permitted to be sewn on so poorly that they fall off the garment while you're carrying it home from the store? Hooks and eyes to be fastened on so insecurely that they drop off the first time you wear them?

✠

Get your children out of the habit of expecting a gift every time you come home from a trip or evening out. They'll be just as happy, and you'll cut down dramatically on the amount of junk around your house.

✠

Instead of buying your children a lot of toys that will be quickly broken and forgotten, give them some basic outdoor play equipment: a swing set, sandbox, tricycle, roller skates, ice skates, balls, bicycle, tennis racket.

✠

When a birthday is coming, try to find out what the person really wants. Sometimes we think that it will be more fun for him to be surprised, but so often this ends up with his being disappointed because he didn't get what he was really hoping for, and he doesn't at all want the thing he got.

✠

The dumps of this world are filled with poorly-chosen gifts. In case of doubt, give money or a gift certificate.

How about giving food for a gift? Everyone needs it, it doesn't add extra pollution to the world, and people don't have to find a place for it in the china cupboard or on the wall. If it's something they can't eat, they can always pass it along to a friend.

When your birthday is coming up, think of what things you need and could really use, then get the message out. This can prevent a lot of waste. If there's something you've really wanted and/or needed, why not say so? The givers will probably be especially pleased to be able to give you something you really want.

Why do you spend your money
for that which is not bread?
Isaiah

Some families light the candles on the birthday cake, blow them out almost immediately, then throw them away, still intact. Others save them and use them again.

Cover the birthday cake when everyone's had what they want. Cake dries out very quickly, becomes inedible and is wasted.

Gift wrapping often can be folded up and re-used.

Will the day come when we'll recycle Christmas cards? Many are so beautiful that it's a shame to throw them away.

When you want to take a gift to a neighbor or friend, how about something that you've canned, frozen, or dried yourself? Or some fresh vegetables or fruit from your garden? Or something you've baked? Or some honey from your own hive? These gifts are especially appreciated because you give something of yourself with them—and yet they're not such a large gift that the person feels overwhelmed. It's also easy on your budget, and it can be done without a long, involved shopping trip.

Anyone can go out and spend money; shopping wisely is an art.

The Yard

Grandfather used to call his home his castle. If a person's home is his castle, his yard around it is his dominion—the green space, however small, that looks to him to make of it a fruitful and peaceable kingdom.

A yard can be a microcosm of the world—a small woodland, meadow, and pool set down in one small square in space and time.

A yard provides a place to dig, soft grass for going barefoot, a place for leaves to fall and wait to be raked up, a spot for angleworms to surface after a rain, the smell of freshly-cut grass, a picnic area, growing room for flowers, a footing for trees, support for a barbecue grill, a dissemination point for pungent barbecue smoke, a carillon for bird songs, a place to smell the moist earth after a rain, a source of nectar for the bees, a home for a chipmunk or two.

MAKE YOUR YARD A PLACE OF BEAUTY

No matter how small your yard, you can invite wildlife to visit or even to set up housekeeping. Four things are necessary:

1. *Food.* This can include flowers, nuts, berries, fruits, seeds, and grains.
2. *Water.* This can be anything from a lake or river at the edge of your property to a stream running through it to a man-made pool or a birdbath or a pan of fresh water set out on a window ledge.

3. *Cover*. Birds and animals need protection from the weather and from their natural enemies.

4. *Reproductive area*. Bushes, trees, and birdhouses can provide places for birds and animals to raise their young.

If your yard is not large enough to offer all four, offer what you can —even a windowbox can provide food and water. If your apartment is not too high above the ground and if you can open one of the windows, try putting out some food and water for the birds. They may make a visit to your windowbox a regular part of their day's routine.

If you have small children or a shut-in in your home, watching birds, squirrels, and other creatures eating lunch at your feeders can be a big part of their day. It's fun for anyone, for that matter; the wildlife are the stars and you're the audience.

For a special treat for the birds, save the fat when you prepare beef. They'll enjoy the raw fat—or you can pour the melted fat into a container, let it harden, and set it out for them.

Your yard is the one spot in all the universe that you have complete (or almost complete) control over; it's your chance to show that this can be a beautiful world if we give it a chance.

First, if your yard is bare you'll need to do some planting. Plantings of shrubbery and flowers around the foundation of the house (with perhaps some vegetables mixed in for variety and as a source of food) can greatly enhance the appearance and the value of your home.

Then you'll need to consider some trees for shade, perhaps some bushes to give privacy between your yard and the next, and some shrubbery to add color, variety, and contrast to your plantings.

Whenever possible, instead of selecting trees and bushes that are purely ornamental (such as lindens and lilacs), choose some that will provide the family with fruits, nuts, or berries. It's surprising how much food one yard can produce if it's given a chance.

If your space is very limited, you might want to try espaliering some trees—training them to grow flat against a wall or in an ornamental design. This works best with dwarf pear and dwarf apple trees. It's fun to do, delightful to look at, and it's a source of edible fruit. All you need is a little space along a wall of the house or garage or on a fence.

• • •

Start a mini-refuge for wildlife in your back yard, no matter how small.

John Strohm

PRUNING AND SHAPING

In order to look their best, most plants need some pruning and shaping. For flowering plants this includes removing faded flowers to encourage the development of more blossoms. Plants such as geraniums, pansies, and trailing petunias that tend to produce long trailing stems should be pruned back regularly for the same reason. Regular pruning during the summer can help shape many plants.

Trees that lose their leaves should be pruned early in the spring before the new growth starts. But spring-flowering shrubs should not be pruned until after they've finished blooming to prevent their becoming overgrown.

Evergreens are usually pruned after the new spring growth has hardened; this helps them keep their formal appearance. But if heavy pruning is necessary, it should be done in the very early spring so that the new growth can fill in the empty spaces in the plant.

Be sure plants get the water they need, especially when they're first planted. If you cover the soil around them with a good layer of mulch, they won't dry out so fast, the soil will be kept from being compacted by frequent waterings or heavy rains, and weeds will not be competing with them for water and nourishment.

 When the well's dry, we know the worth of water.
Benjamin Franklin

CARE OF PLANTS IN CONTAINERS

If you have plants in movable containers, move them to protected areas before storms to keep them from being damaged by wind, rain, and hail. During periods of prolonged heat and drouth move them into semi-shade to prevent severe drying of the soil and the plants.

Plants that require full shade or full sun may need to be moved as the sun patterns change during the growing season. Some plants such as geraniums or petunias may stop blooming if they are left in shaded locations for too long.

In spring and fall when frost is predicted, the containers can be moved into protected areas.

When you go on vacation, move the containers into a protected area and ask a neighbor or friend to water them regularly.

As winter approaches, make sure that all the plants you want to live through the winter have enough moisture in the soil around them. This is especially important for planters containing perennials, evergreens, or deciduous trees and shrubs. Be sure that the soil is thoroughly moistened before the temperature drops below freezing. These will do best if they're moved to a protected area such as an outdoor storage space or a light, cool garage.

During warm periods in the winter, check these containers and water them if the soil is not frozen and is dry. A layer of mulch will help keep the moisture in.

If you use wooden planters for annuals such as petunias, leave the dirt in them over the winter, or the wood will dry and shrink and they will fall apart.

Ceramic, plastic, or metal containers should be emptied and turned upside down if they are to be stored in a cold place to keep water from freezing in them and causing damage.

I am the vine, you are the branches. He that abides in me and I in him, the same brings forth much fruit.

Jesus

CARE OF THE LAWN

Grass is not as fragile as we sometimes think. It can take a lot of dry weather. So in these days of water shortages, don't be too concerned if your grass gets brown and you can't do a thing about it. As soon as there's a good rain, it should be back again, green and lush and clamoring to be cut. You may even start wishing it wouldn't grow so fast.

And you will have saved a lot of water—a lawn can easily soak up 30,000 gallons a year (90,000 gallons in the drier parts of the country).

In the past a velvety green lawn was the mark of a person who cared about his home and neighborhood. But this may change. In the future a lawn that is brown now and then may be the badge of the person who is concerned about our environment, the mark of the person who cares more about the well-being of his friends and neigh-bors than about his grass being uninterruptedly green.

If you do plan to water, check the weather report first. Rain may be on the way.

Weeds can be a problem in a lawn—and usually are. Some have deep or spreading rootstocks that make eradication difficult; others have seeds that can live for a long time in the soil, waiting for the proper conditions to burst forth and grow.

The best way to outwit the weeds is to grow such a vigorous turf that the weed seeds can't germinate—a healthy turf can make weed-killers unnecessary.

Many weeds can be cut or pulled out. And cutting the grass no shorter than 1¾ inches can create enough shade to prevent the germi-nation of the seeds of some kinds of weeds.

But you may need to use some weedkiller to get some weeds out so you can get the grass seed and fertilizer down to the soil. Use as little as you possibly can, however; these chemicals can wash down into nearby waterways and cause a lot of trouble.

First you'll need to identify the weeds that are plaguing you. Your hardware store probably has pictures of the most common ones in your area and can advise you what to use. Or you can get a booklet from your county agent giving a detailed description of what to do for each.

When you buy grass seed, read the label to be sure that no tall fescue is included in the mixture. Red fescue is very good in a lawn, but tall fescue is coarse, tends to fall over and escape the mower, and crowds out the finer grasses. It's often used for football fields and playgrounds, but it looks too coarse in home lawns. You can pull out the clumps of tall fescue if you already have some in your lawn and reseed with something better.

When you buy a new lawnmower, pick out the quietest one available —especially if you like to cut the grass early in the morning. But noise pollution is unwelcome any time of day, so keep your mower as quiet as you can by keeping it in good repair.

If you have a small yard, a lawnmower powered solely by you will use no fuel, cause no air pollution, and give you some of the exercise we all need.

LAWN FURNITURE AND EQUIPMENT

Aluminum lawn furniture can be rewebbed when the original webs give way. This is easy and inexpensive.

Lining the bottom of your grill with gravel or some other material will keep the hot coals from burning it out.

When you've finished cooking on the grill, drop the briquets into a coffee can and put the lid on; this will extinguish them so they can be used again.

If you leave your grill outside, be sure to drain it after each rain to keep it from rusting out—or drill some holes in the bottom to accomplish the same thing.

If your wooden picnic table is getting splintery, give it a coat of stain. This can prolong its life and make picnickers much more comfortable.

Be careful not to leave pieces of equipment such as rakes and hoes outdoors when you're done with them. Their handles can weather quickly in the rain and give you slivers. And they can get rusty.

If the handle on a shovel or other lawn tool breaks, new ones are available at hardware stores.

Keep all tools clean and dry to prevent rusting.

Unless your hands are very tough, you'll probably want to wear gloves to prevent blisters when you rake or hoe.

A lawn can be a lot of work but it can also be a real source of pleasure, of exercise for little-used muscles, and of therapy for tired minds. If everyone had a place to do a little digging, our world would probably be much more relaxed.

The Community

At the turn of the century grandfather could climb the highest hill on his farm, look out over his fields of ripening grain, and breathe the fresh country air. Far below him a stream wound its way through his meadow to the lake where he often fished. There the water was so clear that he could see the bottom many feet down and the fish swimming among the seaweed.

Will we be able to clean up our country so that we can once again enjoy air, water, and land that are clean and healthy? We can if we make the effort, and the time to make that effort is now. As Shirley Temple Black says, "It will be easier and cheaper now and in the next few years than it will be in ten or fifteen years when things are really going to be rough unless something is done today."

LAND

When new parking areas are laid out in your community, see that they aren't entirely blacktop or concrete. Make them attractive and part of nature by creating spaces for trees and bushes. If green growing things produce the oxygen so essential for our existence, when the whole earth is paved over, what are we going to breathe?

✣

Hell is not paved over with good intentions; it's just paved over.

✠

Make sure that trees are given a place in your downtown area. Minneapolis has closed its busiest downtown street to auto traffic and used the space to create a green area with grass and trees and flowers. The human spirit can not live by concrete alone.

✠

Encourage your community to use sand instead of salt on streets and sidewalks. Salt eats into cars and concrete and eventually kills off life in the waters and makes the land desolate.

✠

Unsightly areas such as junkyards that can't be removed can be hidden behind fences and trees. But hopefully we'll soon make cars that last longer, preventing this terrible waste.

✠

Has anyone in your community done anything about the jungle of signs at the edge of town? They add little in the way of beauty and tranquility.

✠

There should be a bill of rights for land on which new construction is going on. In Mineola, New York, bulldozer operators and construction workers have been given these guidelines:

Disturb trees, shrubs, topsoil and groundcover only when absolutely necessary.

Protect the natural surface drainage of water.

Limit noise and unsightliness.

Hold down air pollution.

Notify authorities if potential environmental damage seems imminent.

✠

Streets should be laid out to conform to the topography; otherwise there can be erosion and drainage problems. Paved-over areas present problems because they no longer offer a place for rain water to soak in.

✠

Don't let industries in your community say they can't cut down on the pollution they create—or that in the future they're going to have to cause more pollution. Around the country many companies have found that when they put their minds to finding a solution, they often have discovered ways of using waste materials they previously dumped into the water or onto the land or released into the air. And by finding a new use for what were formerly pollutants, they've increased their profits.

✠

> Sensible people find nothing useless.
> La Fontaine

Dow Chemical announced last year that it expected to make *higher* profits because it was recycling energy and waste materials to meet pollution standards.

✝

It's time that we as communities make a list of all our problems, then check to see if we could match up some of the problems as solutions for others. For instance, the problem of where to dispose of garbage could be solved by pairing it with the problem of how to restore strip-mined land: compost the garbage and work it into the soil. Or the garbage problem might be paired with that of the fuel shortage: burn the garbage as fuel in a plant that creates electricity.

✠

In our throw-away society we've thrown away much of what we now need. If we're going to maintain a good standard of living, we're going to have to start recycling many things.

✠

Has your community set up recycling centers for paper, metals, glass?

✠

What do stores in your community do with all the cardboard boxes they get merchandise in?

✝

Young people in school, church, and community groups that have cleaned up litter in parks and along roads and rivers have learned something about caring for the environment—and hopefully the adults who've watched them have, too.

✠

Youngsters might want to start a recycling project at church or school. Paper, aluminum cans, and returnable bottles are good places to start.

✝

Does your family regularly stack its newspapers for recycling?

✝

If you've ever flown over your community at a low altitude in a small plane and had a good look at your own yard, you'll never dump trash on an unused corner of your property again. From the air every detail shows.

✠

Don't throw out old toys, furniture, appliances, or other household items. Every community has a non-profit organization that gives jobs to the handicapped repairing and selling these things. Your gift will help the repairer, the sales personnel, and the low-income purchaser as well as helping the environment by not asking it to come up with the raw materials and energy to make a new item.

✠

Our society has many customs that are needlessly wasteful: the extra envelope inside a wedding invitation, the two wrappers around some loaves of bread, the newspapers and magazines that try to outdo each other in size. The old saying is especially true today: good things come in small packages.

✠

Try to buy things packaged in paper rather than in plastic. Paper can be recycled, composted, or decomposed in a landfill.

✠

Some cities compost their garbage, mixing it with a little soil and letting it decompose into a light, rich, workable soil, then package it and sell it for lawns and gardens.

✠

The Netherlands is composting 20% of its garbage. If an entire country can do this, why not a city or town?

✠

Some cities have set up community gardens in which people can grow vegetables for their family, putting otherwise unused land to good use; giving people fresh air, exercise, and sunshine; helping families with their food budgets; and increasing the food supply.

✠

Every year more and more acres of good farmland are turned into housing tracts. We now have 2.6 acres of agricultural land per person. At the rate we're turning farmland into shopping centers, home sites, and highways, by the year 2000 we'll only have 1.2 acres of agricultural land per person. To maintain a good diet, 2.2 acres is considered essential. We're the breadbasket of the world, the nation on whom the hungry world is depending to prevent future famines. Can we go on taking more farmland out of production?

We're going to have to start spreading our cities upward instead of outward, switching from sprawling homes with large yards to town-houses and apartments, in order to have enough farmland left for food production.

Perhaps we'll need to amend our building codes to limit the size of new homes. This could conserve many resources.

Unless we limit the size of our families, all the savings we make in energy and resources will quickly be offset.

We can't go on building more and more roads and highways; already we have one mile of road and its right-of-way for every square mile in this country. The new interstate highway system has used up more land than the entire state of Rhode Island. There must be an end to road building and a turn to public transportation.

Perhaps lower fares on public transportation would encourage more people to use it.

Our government now provides funds for highways and air travel; if it diverted some of this money to mass transit, our environment could be greatly helped.

> Whoever has this world's goods and sees his brother in need and does not help him, does the love of God dwell in him?
>
> John

WATER

Be sure private septic tank systems in your area aren't draining into lakes. Back in the day when there were only three or four cottages on a lake, this might not have made any difference, but now that the shores are crowded with homes, lakes can be killed off in a few years by the over-fertilizing that these systems produce.

※

See that businesses—including feedlots—aren't dumping wastes into your lakes and rivers. This can be a good project for a club. Many areas have laws against this that need only to be enforced.

✛

European paper mills have found that they can recycle materials that they were formerly dumping into waterways. By turning them into high protein animal feed they are now making a good profit on what they used to throw away, and the environment is better off for it.

✛

The European Community has adopted a principle regarding who must pay for the cost of cleaning up pollution: "The polluter must pay." Many industries that had been polluting for years and thought that that was the only way they could make a profit are suddenly discovering new ways to use waste products—and often making more profit as a result.

※

We need to set up better guidelines for the use of the oceans by the nations of this world. These will need to include:
1. Fishing rights
2. Mineral and related rights
3. Prevention of pollution

※

What kinds of chemicals are added to your city's water? How high is the bacteria count? Looking into this might be a good project for a group.

AIR

If you see smokestacks pouring pollution into the air in your community, get some local group you belong to—Women's Club, Council of Churches or Sportsmen's Club—to look into this and see why they're being allowed a variance to allow them to go on doing this, then work to get them to clean it up.

✛

General Motors, afraid of what the gasoline shortage can do to the sale of their automobiles, has come up with a unique method of burning coal cleanly in their plants. They've offered to share this process with American industry, hoping a lot of industries will burn coal with this new method instead of burning oil as they previously did, leaving more oil and gasoline for the cars GM builds.

The city of London, once famous (or infamous) for its fog, now has gone so far in cleaning up its air that winter sunshine has increased 50%. Since the 1200s Londoners had been suffering from pollution caused by coal smoke. Now, since the passage of the Clean Air Act, smoke from home chimneys has dropped to 13% of what it was in 1952, and smoke from factory chimneys is down to 18% of what it was then.

In London, 50,000 electric vehicles are used for making deliveries, greatly reducing pollution. Electric cars and trucks might be a help to our cities.

In the same way that railroads are required to switch from diesel fuel to electric power before entering a city, buses and trucks could be required to finish their run into the city with the help of electric power.

If things are allowed to go on as they are, by 1985 air pollution will be reducing the amount of sunlight reaching the earth by one-half. No one has any idea what this will mean to field crops and to all the other green things growing on this earth.

Automobiles produce 90% of all the carbon monoxide in our air.

Lung disease is the fastest growing disease in this country.

The carbon monoxide level on many expressways during rush hours is often above the danger level, impairing the judgment of drivers.

In Los Angeles fifteen percent of the population shows measurable respiratory distress from air pollution—700,000 people in one city.

In the past we took the air and land and water for granted, but we can no longer do this; now we must clean up the damage and begin keeping the environment clean and livable.

✠

Noise causes problems for many city dwellers. Children living on the lower floors of city apartment buildings—nearer the street and street noise—have been found to have considerably more hearing loss and do significantly poorer in school than those living on the higher floors.

✠

Lord Gladwyn, Deputy Leader of the Liberal party in the British House of Lords, believes that the United States will have the greatest difficulty of all the industrialized nations in heading off its "clearly irrational rush to destruction."

He predicts that a United Western Europe will demonstrate to the world how nations can live within their resources.

The Russians and Chinese, he says, will have the easiest time because they're more self-sufficient and more used to being told what standards they must live up to. He says that the Chinese government is well aware of two of the long-term dangers inherent in the Western way of life: pollution and the appalling waste of essential raw materials.

He gives a sober warning: "The U.S. is where the industrial revolution has reached its culmination and where it will undoubtedly destroy itself—and perhaps all of us . . . if it is allowed to proceed unhindered."

✠

We're all hoping *somebody else* will do something about pollution.

✠

We're all for clean air, water, and land, but we hate to think of the cost. But in the long run, once we get the environment cleaned up, we'll enjoy longer lives and better health—and begin *saving* money.

✠

We used to think that growth was essential for a city, that the city that wasn't growing was dying; now we know that growth can bring many problems.

Cities must set up standards that will make sure growth is not at the expense of the quality of life.

✠

We must not use the Gross National Product as a measure of the good life; fewer goods, but better, healthier living conditions would be a wiser measurement.

We need to develop a whole new way of looking at things, of considering first the well-being of people and of the environment we live in. As Shirley Temple Black has said, "We need to develop a new ethic as a nation, and this ethic is going to have to operate at all levels of government, individual, and private life."

He that giveth unto the poor shall not lack.
Proverbs

The Abundant Life

Long before the white man came, when the Indian roamed this land, the air was clean and fresh, the rivers and lakes sparkled, and the soil was eager to produce.

It can be that way again—if we're willing to put things back in order and start living the kind of life that will keep them that way.

The problem is that we will each have to begin doing this now, not waiting until we see everyone else doing it first. A leader says, "I will live this way because it is right"; a follower says, "I'll wait to see what other people do." We must be leaders.

Some people say, "Technology got us into this situation so technology can get us out of it. I'm not going to change my way of living one bit."

Others will admit that we have also been wasteful and try to live less wastefully.

Some people will kick and scream and act childish as they experience shortages.

Others will look for ways of managing that don't depend so much on these scarce items.

Some people will keep on using more and more electricity, adding more appliances and gadgets each year.

Others will try to learn to live in ways that use less fuel.

Some people will let the scarcity of some items make them more grasping and selfish.

Others will learn the joy of sharing.

Some people will say, "I can't do it! I can't change my way of living."

Others will gradually adjust and enjoy learning to make do with what they have.

Some people will let standards for clean air and water be lowered.

Others will realize that our health need not be sacrificed for our industries, that industry already has ways of cutting down on the pollution it causes.

Some people will say, "Well, this is the end of the good life."

Others will realize that *things* are not what make life good.

Couldn't we as a people

- set restrictions on the weight and the gas consumption of new automobiles?
- set mandatory insulation standards for new buildings?
- eliminate throwaway containers?
- start using some of our highway trust funds to improve our mass transit systems since we won't be using our highways as much as we used to?
- do away with all incentives that make it cheaper to use more instead of less electricity?
- insist that more of our trucking be switched to the rails?
- urge our congressmen to work for legislation to improve our air, water, and soil?
- give top priority to researching and developing cleaner sources of energy such as geothermal, solar, and fusion—sources that will not be quickly exhausted?

Do we really need

- three cars per family—or two—or even one?
- to travel so much?
- as many new clothes?
- as much packaging on the goods we buy?
- so many *things* of all sorts?

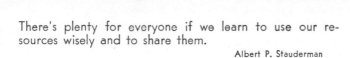

There's plenty for everyone if we learn to use our resources wisely and to share them.

Albert P. Stauderman

Can't we do away with

- hunger and malnutrition?
- built-in obsolescence in cars, appliances and other manufactured items?
- the idea that bigger is better?

The spoiled person

- demands the whole bag of candy, leaving none for anyone else.
- breaks his toys, throws them away, then asks for more.
- purposely scuffs his shoes as he walks, saying, "My mother will buy me more."
- expects someone else to clean up after him.
- cries if he has to do without something.
- is rarely thankful for what he already has.
- demands more of everything.
- insists that he must have the finest of everything.
- is not at all aware of the needs of those around him.
- wants what he wants when he wants it.
- doesn't care if he ruins things for the next person who must use them.
- thinks the world owes him everything.
- blames other people for all his problems.
- throws a tantrum if everything doesn't go his way.
- will stop at nothing to get what he wants.
- will not inconvenience himself in the slightest to help someone else.
- feels sorry for himself if things are not perfect.
- laughs at those who are not as well off as he is.
- insists that he has to have a certain thing, but doesn't appreciate it when he gets it.
- thinks that he is the only one that matters in the whole world.

The mature person

- knows that the people around him have needs too.
- takes care of what he has.
- doesn't expect anyone to clean up after him.
- shares what he has.
- is concerned about other people's problems.
- doesn't expect to have everything he might like.
- appreciates what he has.
- doesn't expect everyone to give him everything.
- doesn't spoil things for those who'll be coming after him.
- is willing to work and wait for things.
- doesn't expect to have more than his share.
- doesn't blame others for all his problems.
- realizes that other people have rights.
- takes responsibility.
- tries to do his share.

This can be a time of

- appreciating what we have.
- getting to know our neighbors better.
- enjoying our family more.
- getting to know the area around us.
- developing our creativity.

If we're really concerned we'll

- realize that this world's resources are limited.
- begin living as mature, responsible people.
- work to make our world a fit place for our children and their children after them.

We must not sacrifice the environment to meet the energy crisis in the United States.

Norman Cousins

When Jesus said that he had come so that we might have life more abundantly, he didn't mean he had come to make us rich in *things*. He had in mind more important matters such as:

- realizing we are loved and accepted by God, just as we are, right now.
- accepting this most wonderful gift.
- living it toward others.

We will try to

- Use no more than our share.
- See that everyone gets his share.
- Keep things in balance, putting back as well as taking out.
- Leave the world in good shape for those who will come after us.

We must replace materialism with a reverence for life in all its forms—we must reclaim the land—we must purify the air and waterways.

John B. Harrison